YOGA SUTRAS SIMPLIFIED

YOGA SUTRAS
SIMPLIFIED

A Soul-Searching Adventure with Patanjali

VASUDEV MURTHY

JAICO PUBLISHING HOUSE

Ahmedabad Bangalore Chennai
Delhi Hyderabad Kolkata Mumbai

Published by Jaico Publishing House
A-2 Jash Chambers, 7-A Sir Phirozshah Mehta Road
Fort, Mumbai - 400 001
jaicopub@jaicobooks.com
www.jaicobooks.com

YOGA SUTRAS SIMPLIFIED
ISBN 978-93-93559-45-6

First Jaico Impression: 2022

Page design and layout by
Special Effects Graphics Design Company, Mumbai

Printed by
Gopsons Papers Pvt. Ltd., Noida, (U.P.)

योगेन चित्तस्य पदेन वाचां
मलं शरीरस्य च वैद्यकेन।
योऽपाकरोत्तं प्रवरं मुनीनां
पतञ्जलिं प्राञ्जलिरानतोऽस्मि ॥

Yōgēna cittasya padēna vācāṁ
malaṁ śarīrasya ca vaidyakēna.
Yōpākarōttaṁ pravaraṁ munīnāṁ
patañjaliṁ prāñjalirānatōsmi

I bow with my hands together to the eminent sage Patanjali,
who removed the impurities of the mind through yoga,
of speech through grammar,
and of the body through medicine.

Bhoja Rājamārttanda

I know a little girl who speaks with her late great-grandfather every night with the purest of love.

They have a shared consciousness.

This book is dedicated to that little girl.

Foreword

Yogacharya Dr. Ananda Balayogi Bhavanani, MBBS, MD, C-IAYT, DSC

Director, Centre for Yoga Therapy, Education and Research (CYTER) of Sri Balaji Vidyapeeth and Chairman, International Centre for Yoga Education and Research (ICYER) at Ananda Ashram, Puducherry (Pondicherry), India

Maharishi Patanjali is one of the greatest ever humane beings to have walked this planet. To me he is a time traveller, a being from the future who, in his benevolence, blesses humanity from time to time with his timeless teachings. "Superman Pat", as I lovingly refer to him, has shown us that we human beings are nothing but the Cosmic Being Ishwara bewildered by amnesia. We, who have forgotten who we truly are, need to be reminded that all we need to do is clear away the debris and regain that original state of "Oneness", which is our Essential Nature.

Yoga Darshan is the reverential perspective of reality that has been codified by this greatest of sages through his phenomenal *Yoga Sutras*. These 196 terse verses must have been composed and then transmitted by the oral tradition from at least 1500–1000 BC but came into the written form much later, around 500 BC–AD 300. The sutras were always kept short, as they were intended to be learnt, memorised and chanted with reverence and understanding in order to facilitate the development of a deep sense of quiet and inner contemplation.

The Yoga Sutras are arranged in a logical form and placed in four chapters.

Section 1: Samadhi Pada

Patanjali starts with the definition of yoga as a process of mental purification. It is the classical definition of yoga as a discipline to control the whirlpools of the subconscious or unconscious mind.

Maharishi Patanjali stresses the importance of *abhyasa* (practice) and the profound concept of *vairagya* (dispassionate objectivity) when he says that mental fluctuations will cease on their own accord once one has perfected these twin keys.

Patanjali deals with the concept of samadhi, classifying it into numerous levels and sublevels, emphasising the essential qualities needed for attainment. There are many obstacles on the yogic path to *kaivalya* (liberation) and solutions to these as well.

Once we stabilise the restless mind, it attains the highest clarity and becomes crystal-like in its ability to truthfully transmit the highest experiences.

Section 2: Sadhana Pada

Patanjali begins with a description of the process of gradual disengagement from karmic bondage. According to Sage Vasishtha, *Atma Jnana* (knowledge of the Self) is the only way we can escape from the clutches of the never-ending cycle of births. Patanjali echoes this when he says that only the wise one endowed with *viveka* (discerning intellect) can see clearly that all worldly experiences are ultimately nothing but suffering and pain. It is only the highest state of kaivalya that is the real bliss, and anything less is pain, according to Patanjali. This is similar in many ways to the core of the Buddhist philosophy that views all life as suffering.

Patanjali advises us to prevent those miseries that are yet to occur, a vital clue about the importance of preventive action in avoiding future sorrow. He further states that the cause of pain is the union between the seer and the seen.

The real purpose of yoga sadhana is expressed when he states that the sustained practice of the various limbs of yoga is meant for the destruction of the impurities, thus enabling one to cultivate the highest wisdom of enlightenment. To this end, he enumerates the eight-fold royal path of Ashtanga Yoga.

He further advises us to cultivate *pratipaksha bhavana*, the contrary view when one is faced with negative thoughts that cause suffering. I have personally found that a strong "STOP" statement works wonders in helping to block out the negative thoughts that otherwise lead us into the quicksand of deeper trouble.

Patanjali defines asana as a state that radiates stability and ease. Such a state may be attained only through regular disciplined and determined practice. The key to attaining this state is to practise asana with a relaxation of effort and contemplation of the infinite.

Pranayama is defined as the "cessation of the processes of inhalation and exhalation". Such a state of going beyond the breath is another example of Patanjali's genius in explaining the higher concepts with simplicity. When faced with something that amazes us, we say, "It took my breath away!" Imagine, then, the state of our breath when we are face-to-face with the divine experience itself! Having described pranayama as a bridge between the external and internal worlds, he goes on to define *pratyahara* as the "withdrawing of the mind from the sensory engagements". Just as a tortoise withdraws its limbs into its shell, the senses cease to function as soon as the mind (the main energy source for sensory function) starts the journey inwards.

Section 3: Vibhuti Pada

Now ready for the onward inner journey, Patanjali starts the third pada, giving definitions of the three internal aspects (*antaranga*) of yoga, namely *dharana*, dhyana and samadhi. He defines dharana as the process of binding consciousness to a point, place, region or object and dhyana as the state in which there is a steady and continuous flow of attention and concentration to a point, place, region or object.

The state of absorptive super-consciousness (samadhi) is an omnipresent state in which the mind loses itself, and the object alone shines without differentiation. These three internal limbs are known together as *samyama* (flowing together seamlessly). He describes the special experiences and powers (siddhis) that result from performing samyama on various gross and subtle objects. It is important to note that he warns us that the siddhis are both an attainment as well as an obstacle to spiritual progress.

Section 4: Kaivalya Pada

This chapter has a mere 34 verses, but Patanjali gives us piercing insights into that highest state of liberation known as kaivalya. He examines the concept of karma and describes the relationship between action and reaction. He discusses the concept of reincarnation when he states that the deep habit patterns (samskaras) have an unbroken continuity and play out from lifetime to lifetime by giving rise to the different types of incarnations, locations and time frames.

He gives us an excellent concept of the threefold nature of time when he says that the past and future both exist in the present reality but appear different only because of their distinctive characteristics and forms.

Patanjali helps us understand the concept of gunas by explaining that they are the backbone of all that manifests as well as that which is at subtle planes of existence. He tells us how the same object may be perceived differently by different minds because the minds themselves manifest differently. No wonder everyone seems to have their own view of the world!

The discriminating mind now begins to gravitate towards absolute liberation from all experiences that otherwise result because of the interaction between the seer and the seen. With the final frontier being conquered, we become the Divine itself in the state of kaivalya. We lose our sense of individuality in order to gain a sense of absolute universality.

This inspiring interpretation by Sri Vasudev Murthy, *Yoga Sutras Simplified: A Soul-Searching Adventure with Patanjali*, is a much-needed literary contribution at this point in time as the youth of the world are seeking answers on their terms.

The young reader, more often than not, seeks a condensed and distilled form of wisdom. They want to have answers to their questions and often focus on "What is in it for me?" The longer we prolong the "take-aways", the higher the chances that they will move on, feeling that such teachings are impractical or are esoteric material with little or no relevance to their fast-paced lives.

It is a well-accepted fact that each of the sutras can be expanded into multiple PhD dissertations. However, the challenge in presenting any interpretation of these teachings is to group such complex verses in a simple and digestible manner without compromising their essence. This is the acid test for every modern writer who seeks to share the timeless wisdom contained in the great traditional texts of *Sanathana Dharma*.

In our many discussions over the past year, I have found that Murthyji has taken on the self-responsibility to make each and every reader comfortable with the subject. To this end, he uses all the tricks of his trade as a writer, be it his personal anecdotes, the numerous enthralling stories, or the contemporary analogies that embellish every page and make the reader feel at ease. Through all these priceless, timeless methods, he takes the reader on a remarkable journey, one of the "Self to the Self, through the Self".

Contents

Foreword ix
Introduction 1

Section I The Merger—Samadhi Pada **13**
1 Stilling the Mind for the Journey Inwards 15
2 Mastering the Distractions to Access the Rewards 43

Section 2 The Discipline—Sadhana Pada **67**
3 Tuning the Engine of the Mind 69
4 Engineering the Mind and Body 101

Section 3 The Power—Vibhuti Pada **137**
5 Exploring Mental Alchemy 139
6 Mastering the Elements 169

Section 4 The Isolation—Kaivalya Pada **197**
7 The Path to Convergence 199
8 The Brilliance of Solitude 223

Distilling the Yoga Sutras 237
Acknowledgements 249
Appendix 253

पातञ्जलयोगसूत्राणि 253
॥ प्रथमोऽध्यायः ॥ ॥ समाधि-पादः ॥ (Samadhi Pada) 253
॥ द्वितीयोऽध्यायः ॥ ॥ साधन-पादः ॥ (Sadhana Pada) 257
॥ तृतीयोऽध्यायः ॥ ॥ विभूति-पादः ॥ (Vibhuti Pada) 261
॥ चतुर्थोऽध्यायः ॥ ॥ कैवल्य-पादः ॥ (Kaivalya Pada) 265

Introduction

What a great country we live in!

Breathe the air, drink the water from its rivers! Revel in the chaos! Be ecstatic about its food! Enjoy its beautiful and thrilling festivals!

And how could I forget its music! I know that the music of this country speaks of thousands of years of culture and knowledge. Of the melodies of the land, of holy rivers, of the monsoon!

A country that gave rise to great philosophical and spiritual insights.

And yoga.

Yes. That breathtaking heritage of humanity called yoga!

You may be aware that yoga is one of our greatest contributions to the world. It is synonymous with India and gives our country a level of respect that others do not command.

Everyone's heard of yoga. There are yoga studios and schools everywhere, offering every possible variant of yoga. "You must do yoga" is common advice, handed out to someone who looks stressed and unfit. There's even an International Day of Yoga—June 21!

But wait!

Is that really yoga? All those twists and turns and bends—really?

The answer is: Yes, but it's a little more complex than that. A lot more complex.

Let's find out.

First, some background. You should know a little about Patanjali before we continue because it is his critical thinking and commentary that we shall be deconstructing in this book. Here was someone who brought together and organised the entire philosophy of yoga into a systematic structure that could be studied, assimilated and acted upon.

Some say Patanjali lived about 2,500 years ago. In our lore, he is one of 18 *siddhas*, a term for perfected masters who were said to have achieved a high degree of physical and spiritual perfection. He wrote the Yoga Sutras, a magnificent classical text on yoga, which is a critical foundational piece of Indic culture and thought. "Sutras" means threads, by the way.

The story of Patanjali traces back to a celestial incident. Adisesha, a serpent with a thousand heads, prayed to Vishnu to be reborn so he could learn the art of dance from Shiva.

He wanted to see Shiva perform in Chidambaram, once called Thillai, in Tamil Nadu, a state in southern India.

An aged yogini, Gonika, was praying to the sun, seeking a son to pass on her knowledge to before she died. She offered water in her cupped palms to the sun.

Adisesha fell into her palms from the heavens as a small snake and took human form. Gonika was taken aback and dropped him. That is how he got his name: *Pat*—fallen, *Anjali*—folded palms.

Patanjali is depicted as someone with his lower limbs coiled like a snake. Unusual and a bit macabre but all in a day's work for our charming Indian stories. No one with an appreciation for our ethos would bat an eyelid; it seems perfectly plausible.

He is said to have watched a magnificent dance competition between Shiva and Parvati. Shiva, in the form of Nataraja, won. Parvati, as Kali, was defeated and moved to a temple on the outskirts of the town of Chidambaram. The main temple, considered to have been consecrated by Patanjali, celebrates the dancing Nataraja. (It's a gorgeous temple, incidentally. Do visit!)

It is not a flight of imagination to believe that Patanjali was inspired by Nataraja.

In fact, Nataraja has been a source of inspiration for many art forms and philosophies. For instance, Bharatanatyam, the great classical dance of India, always starts with an invocation to Nataraja. And at the European Council for Nuclear Research (CERN), a high-energy physics laboratory in Switzerland, there is a statue of Nataraja because of its esoteric significance relating to the cosmic dance and its connection to CERN's study of subatomic particles.

Physicist Fritjof Capra explains in *The Tao of Physics*:

> "The Dance of Shiva symbolises the basis of all existence. At the same time, Shiva reminds us that the manifold forms in the world are not fundamental, but illusory and ever-changing."

Patanjali wrote many sophisticated texts of great depth. The popular and hypnotising *Nataraja Stotra* is ascribed to him. He commented authoritatively on medicine and grammar too. But the work he is particularly famous for is the Yoga Sutras, a collection of extremely tight near-aphorisms, or sutras, referring to yoga.

Patanjali was clearly an exalted intellectual with extraordinary powers of comprehension and articulation. He took it upon himself to write down 196 lines of sharp and incisive wisdom. He moved back from the currents of life and explained everything that needed to be explained about existence. What prompted Patanjali to write this text? Was it his own experiences? Or was it an inspired insight into the deepest of fundamentals that explain why we are born and die and what life is all about?

But let's step back for a minute.

Have you considered why you were born?

Why do you have this life? Why do you die? Why do you experience pain, suffering, joy and so on? Why are we consumed by desires and are never satisfied? Have you considered whether there is a final purpose of some kind? Do you wish there were clear and logical indicators of behaviours that would help you live a fulfilling life? Why do you react to situations in the way you do, and how come others react differently? I am sure you have thought about all this.

You are then ready to consider the beauty of the Yoga Sutras, a timeless classic with deep insights into the human mind and behaviour.

As the rays of comprehension fall upon us shortly after we take birth, our bodies (are they ours?) tentatively poke the fabric of illusions, which we mistakenly believe is the "real world". Already born with a fear of death, the sense of identity takes firm root very quickly.

"That is my mother, and she loves me," I say to the universe, and I am swept away by a feeling of intense love, which is this sensation of safety. I crave a toy or a blanket or the sweet taste of my mother's milk. I don't like loud sounds, and I like to stay warm. I fall asleep, and strange, jumbled thoughts from my previous births invade my dreams.

And as I grow, I feel proud of my limbs, my skin, my teeth, my hair, my eyes. I speak, and people respond. In turn, I listen and comprehend. I read, I write, I form opinions. I see beauty. I experience disgust. I love, and I hate. I believe I am very smart and intelligent. And at times, I feel stupid and embarrassed. This is me.

(But who am I?)

All this while, this very body, going through stages of bloom, plateauing and gentle decay, has already been marked for corruption. For my young self, time stretches ahead infinitely. And yet, that future and my past are all latent in this specific moment. Everything is precisely designed!

But as my youth becomes a memory and my body decelerates, there is a slow but discernible increase in anxiety. I shall die. And I am consumed by fear. What does death mean? If there is an "I", will "I" survive? If so, then in what form? Disembodied? A new birth?

If there is finality inherent in death, then what was the point of the life that I lived anyway?

My amorphous mind gravitates to these serious thoughts.

Here is an extract from a story I once wrote called *The Time Merchants* on that theme—the gradual comprehension of our mortality:

> And so, they were born. Again and again. As men and women. They bought Time from us and started the journey. In the beginning, they were cocky and confident with the brashness of infancy and youth. Death seemed distant and not even a possibility. Their parents died, and so did their friends. But they felt they would not, and they were sure about it. They exercised, dieted and prayed. They did whatever it took to develop resistance to death.
>
> So, they struggled. Every now and then, we would send them reminders that Time, that which they

had bought, was ticking away. It was in different forms—a sickness here, a dream there. Resistance was futile. But what do you do when the desire to live forever is so overpowering that it walks over reason? Finally, it would come. The last strand of allocated Time, the last grain, was consumed. Like moths fighting against the lure of light, they fought hard. But there was no way at all that they could be successful.

The love of life and the fear of death pulsate subliminally throughout. A pendulum marks attraction and aversion. I revel in a pool of paper-thin, bogus "knowledge", fertilised by the praise of those who, too, do not know, all the while not understanding that just below lies another pool of truth of infinite depth.

We wonder that we emerged from the darkness, and we also accept that when death arrives, we will once again drown in darkness. What exactly is it? We do not understand it. We do not *wish* to understand it. Our ability to comprehend is meagre.

And so, we get swept away in whatever seems to make sense—the business of living life.

Our mind is always in ferment. When awake or when asleep, our mind trembles and quivers like jelly, constantly dictating our reasoning, our responses, our actions and inactions. Families, career, the making of money, the need to feel appreciated. We, equivalent to twigs, swim feebly in a powerful, massive current, imagining that our individual identity is distinct. It hurts our ego and sense of self to imagine that we are fundamentally inconsequential, not even atoms in a gigantic and infinitely deep ocean of consciousness. Both time and space stretch across a canvas we do not have the mental ability to comprehend.

Patanjali's Yoga Sutras are neatly divided into four sections (padas):

1. Samadhi Pada—which I shall call The Merger—consists of 51 sutras. This pada explains the gradual process of dissolving with the Supreme and understanding the pitfalls and challenges along the way.
2. Sadhana Pada—which I shall call The Discipline—consists of 55 sutras. This pada explains the first five of the eight disciplines needed to attain samadhi. The popular physical aspect of yoga, called asanas, is referred to here.
3. Vibhuti Pada—which I shall call The Power—consists of 56 sutras. This pada expands on the last three of the eight disciplines and speaks of the mystical powers you may achieve during this process.
4. Kaivalya Pada—which I shall call The Isolation—consists of 34 sutras. This pada explains the process of sublimation and profound concepts like time.

You will get to know about these fascinating padas in great detail soon.

This book is an attempt to simplify Patanjali's Yoga Sutras with minimal reference to the Sanskrit texts themselves. The concepts are eternally relevant and are applicable in today's world too. They can give you clear advice and direction as you go through life. The original sutras are available at the end of the book if you wish to read them.

It is important for you to know that asanas (postures)—incorrectly assumed by many to be the entire meaning of yoga—are referred to in a very terse way in the Sadhana Pada section.

Yoga is a term translating roughly to 'the Union'.

With whom, you ask?

With a Supreme Power or Infinite Reality.

Everything emerges from and merges with this entity, which we may have trouble comprehending due to our mental limitations. Nevertheless, most of us acknowledge the existence of such a power, which we believe is the reason we exist in the first place. We find such an explanation plausible. Entire religions have been created on this premise and on how adherents of religions interpret this power. Whether or not this power is benign and caring is a matter to be considered separately.

We thus say that yoga refers to the desirable state of you merging with the Supreme, achieving your life's purpose.

There is a straightforward way to visualise the Supreme to

help you focus while you traverse this book.

Take your awareness between your closed eyes. Imagine then that you are looking through a vast distance at some indeterminate point. Imagine that this indistinct point you are observing with unwavering focus is the Infinite Reality. That is where you wish to go.

Consciously relax the muscles around your eyes, which tend to be in a state of tension without your realising it. This will help you focus even better and clear your forehead. As your mind is assaulted by thoughts, push them away with determination and keep your focus for as long as possible. This can be a helpful mechanism to adopt while reading this book without complicating things too much.

We may further assume that life is a mere flash of awareness between two voids. These voids represent the Supreme or the Infinite Reality, which some feel comfortable calling God.

Patanjali's Yoga Sutras provide a clear direction on merging with the Supreme.

I have divided each section into two chapters in a logical manner. At the end of each chapter, I have talked about the impact that the chapter had on me, as an ordinary person. After each pada, you will see an image filling out, much like a jigsaw puzzle taking shape.

Some words in Sanskrit are difficult to translate correctly and have been left as is. This is not an insurmountable challenge; it is hoped that the context in which they are used will give meaning to such words.

The Yoga Sutras analyse the fickle mind in extraordinary detail and ought to be required reading for psychologists! Patanjali takes us comprehensively through every aspect of the experience of life and helps us make sense of it.

A suggestion for the journey through the book: read a few pages at a time. Stop and reflect on what you have read. Patanjali's Yoga Sutras are a beautiful text that needs to be appreciated a little at a time. Take a break. Come back again.

Now, onwards to the first chapter!

Section I

The Merger—Samadhi Pada

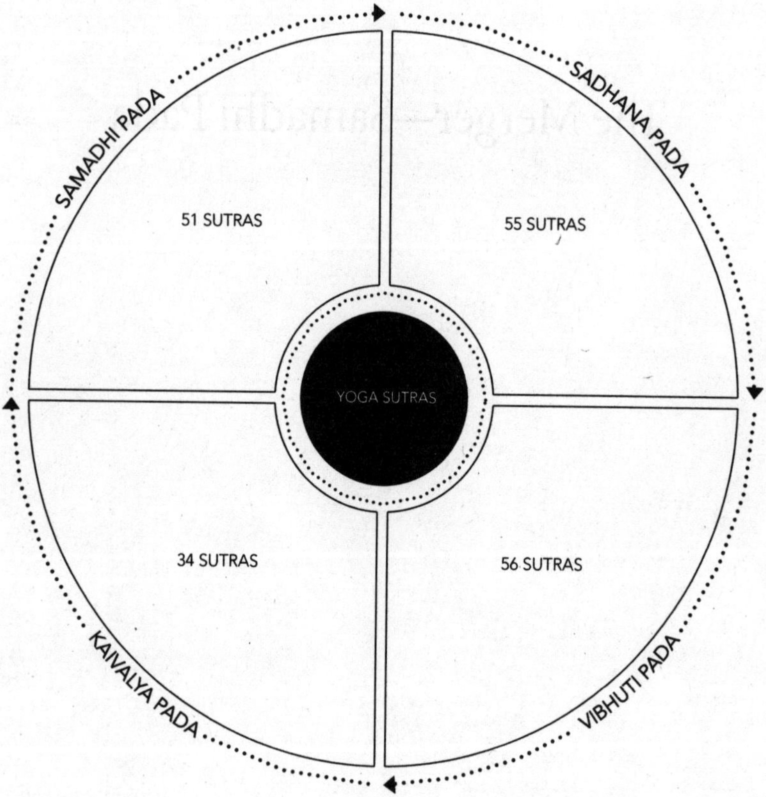
SAMADHI PADA
SADHANA PADA
VIBHUTI PADA
KAIVALYA PADA
51 SUTRAS
55 SUTRAS
34 SUTRAS
56 SUTRAS
YOGA SUTRAS

1

Stilling the Mind for the Journey Inwards

Sutras 1–14

When I was in college at Roorkee and then subsequently through my young adulthood, I went through frequent bouts of ill-health. I was also extremely erratic; I was easily upset and suffered from extended periods of quiet misery. Often angry, and because I was also articulate and spoke with passion about various issues, I managed to get into tense situations. I am a violinist, and this fact unfortunately amplified my reactions to any situation quite unnecessarily, as musicians tend to be "emotional". Some called me a rebel without a cause. It was not a compliment.

On a visit home from college to Bangalore, my father—now deceased—drove me to someone's home. My father said he was a yoga expert, and the interaction might be helpful, though he did not specify why. I understood much later that he wanted me to calm down a little.

I met the gentleman, but he did not leave much of an impression on me. He could not connect with a hypersensitive young man, always on edge. All he did was hand over a book he had written about yoga and ask me to read it. It had several poorly drawn illustrations. The book left absolutely no impression on me.

Life continued. I went to study overseas and worked there as well. For no specific reason that I can recall, after many years, I started attending yoga classes in Dallas run by an Indian immigrant. I enjoyed it to an extent. It was all about physical fitness to me at that time. My mind was still in constant flux, battling various imaginary enemies, at work, at home, in the past and in the future.

One student in those classes stood out. Let's call him Matthew Grimes. He was professionally a barber. In the class, he was quite adept in his asana (physical poses) practice and often assisted the principal instructor.

He was in his late fifties and looked like a sage. Such a peaceful face, such a slow, deliberate way of speaking, such a soft gentleness around him—well, I quite liked him.

As I grew to know Matthew, I came to know that he had had a tumultuous life full of chaos. He had cut and styled the hair of the rich and famous and had been very affluent.

He revealed that he had been involved in a serious car accident a few years prior and was hospitalised for a year. That was a period of intense reflection for him, he said. He could do nothing but that. It dawned on him that his earlier flashy, hedonistic lifestyle was quite pointless.

During this time, he met someone who suggested that yoga may have answers. And thus began his exploration into yoga and meditation. I secretly admired Matthew's stoic nature and wished that I were like him.

But I was still not ready. My yoga sessions were exercises in restless energy. There was incense drifting through the room and soft music in the background. I found them irritating. I scoffed at words used about peace and love; it all seemed artificial and contrived.

I was impatient, waiting for the class to start, waiting for a sequence to finish, waiting for the class to end, waiting to jump into my car and drive off. I was hyper and thought it reflected energy and ambition, which were and continue to be much-admired qualities.

I returned to India after several years but never forgot Matthew. He passed away in 2019. I remember him with respect.

I was older now but not necessarily wiser and continued to surround myself with turbulence, much of it self-created.

My father intervened again, telling me that I ought to investigate yoga. I was in a state of simmering conflict with him, as I was with everyone else, and reacted in a predictably hostile manner. But finally, after much cajoling and with some reluctance, I agreed to enrol in a yoga school near my home in Bangalore.

It was transformative.

The instructors were strict and had no time for pampering anyone with soft words about "getting in touch with their feelings", as you might hear in modern yoga classes. A class of 30 students had to move together in harmony, following terse directions. And yet, in that discipline, I saw that the instructors were at another level. Like Matthew, they too had a certain peace on their faces. But unlike the gentle and reserved Matthew, they spoke firmly but calmly and with clarity. Their spines were erect, and their eyes shone with confidence. They were in control.

I needed all that.

We began our sessions with the Sanskrit prayer to Patanjali that you may have read at the beginning of this book. I'm embarrassed to say that that was the very first time I had heard of Patanjali.

I did very well and became adept at many asanas. I became healthier and relatively more balanced as a person. I had many deeply personal meditative experiences which would follow my intense physical yoga sessions. I loved going to my classes. And my yoga instructors seemed imbued with a certain light and dignity that I was in awe of.

They occasionally made cryptic remarks that the practice of asanas was only a part of yoga. My curiosity was piqued, though I did not act on it. At that time, my objective was to achieve a level of mental balance and physical resilience. I did achieve that objective, though just barely.

Patanjali: Now begins the discipline of yoga.

Deeper exploration followed. I cannot truthfully say that I had read Patanjali's Yoga Sutras at that point and learnt more.

But there was an undercurrent, which manifested in many ways. Indirect allusions in conversations, random quotations—clearly, this was an important text to understand and make sense of as a critical foundational text central to Indian culture and civilisation.

Meanwhile, my violin playing became smoother and slower. I enjoyed dwelling on single musical notes for extended periods. My conflicts with the outer world reduced significantly, though not completely.

It was not that I had not thought about all this earlier. But in my mind, yoga was vaguely all about physical fitness. And as I discovered, that was not the case at all!

Yet, when I finally did read the book, the first brilliant and terse line in Sanskrit by Patanjali hit home. Encapsulated in those syllables was this wisdom:

Yoga is a cessation of the mind reacting to stimulus.

The sharp impact of those lines was phenomenal.

I argued with myself that it was impossible to prevent the mind from reacting to situations. It seemed independent. The mind was me. But it was not me either since I could not control it.

It was confusing.

After deep thought, I arrived at several working definitions of yoga.

- Yoga is the ability to be stoic.
- Yoga is the ability to curb reactions and not allow your mind to be affected.

- Yoga is a larger path to determining one's purpose in life.
- Yoga is about training oneself to work towards a higher goal, removing the cobwebs that cover one's constantly churning mind and go deep within.
- Yoga gives us answers to the question of what the ultimate purpose of this life is.

You too may arrive at your own satisfactory conclusion as you go through this book. But let us get back to what Patanjali has said.

Quieten your mind! Control your mind!

And immediately, we must ask the question:

But what is the mind?

Formally, it is that part of our faculties involved in thinking, understanding and experiencing emotions.

You are constantly engaged with your mind. It defines you in a significant way. This is where the most private of your thoughts reside and where none can enter.

Look inwards.

So much is happening.

Your mind is filled with thoughts, memories, sensations, apprehensions, responses and so much more. Here you will find anger, joy, hope, sadness, alarm, fear, love, regret, despondency and much more. In a constant flux, your mind swirls with thoughts that often come in uninvited, which in turn further perplexes you.

In fact, you may agree that it seems impossible to control your mind. It responds and is constantly active. The slightest perturbation in the environment—mental or physical—causes the mind to react. The more you avoid a thought, the more it intrudes and demands attention.

You often hear people exclaim, "Don't think so much" or "I overthink", etc. But do you really have a say in the matter?

And therefore, Patanjali says, the purpose of yoga is to have such control over your mind that it is indifferent to any tremor or perturbation, internal or external.

And then he says, most profoundly, that

When you can still those thoughts, you will see your true self!

Clouded by thoughts, forever restless, the mind declines to cooperate and be controlled. You are preoccupied with its illogical twists and turns and follow it like a slave. The mind is modified constantly. You are consumed by your changing mind.

Does the mind control you, or do you control the mind?

Yes, you *can* control your mind, says Patanjali.

Once you control it, once you are impervious to mischievous provocations and inducements to modify your mind, that is when you will discover the true YOU.

Patanjali's acute intelligence shines through in his work at every turn. So many centuries before we had management jargon to confuse us, he shone the light on the merits of absolute objectivity and a structured communication style most appropriate for a reader.

He says that to master these modifications of the mind, you need to know what they are before coming up with a plan of action.

We learn that there are five types of mental modifications or alterations, some pleasant or appealing, and some distasteful. These he groups in logical buckets as follows:

- Valid Inference
- Invalid Inference
- Imagination
- Sleep
- Memory

Patanjali's extraordinary brevity encapsulates these beautiful thoughts in two simple lines in the original Sanskrit. You can validate his declaration by looking at any thought that comes to your mind; it will certainly be one of the five types above!

It is perfectly reasonable to ask what each of these terms means.

Patanjali defines *valid inference* in three ways:

ONE: as **direct perception**—how we become aware of something via our senses.

We see two cars in an accident, right in front of us.
There can be no doubt.

TWO: as a **logical inference**—a conclusion based on concrete evidence or irrefutable logic.

> *We see several cars stalled in front of us and are unable to proceed. There is no doubt that there is a roadblock that we can't directly see. Seeing an ambulance drive by towards where the confusion appears to be, we conclude that there has been an accident somewhere ahead.*

THREE: **the word** of someone universally acknowledged as being fair, truthful and consistent.

> *A traffic policeman stops us and says that there has been a car accident a kilometre ahead and advises us to turn back.*

This complete set of *valid* inferences has a clear impact on the mind and *modifies* or *alters* it or causes it to be engaged. The alteration may or may not be pleasing. At any rate, we have been affected.

Next, Patanjali speaks of the second mental modification, namely *invalid inference*.

False knowledge is accumulated due to an incorrect sequence of reasoning. This could be the result of deliberate lies or wrong assumptions about persons, events or objects; these ultimately result in an invalid inference. As a simple example, you may incorrectly deduce that your pocket was picked while you were walking, but in fact, you might have left your wallet at home.

Or consider this: has it happened that you noticed a couple of people looking in your direction and laughing? You incorrectly inferred that they were laughing at you, but perhaps they were laughing at a funny advertisement *behind* you.

As explained above, the untrained mind is forced to respond to invalid inferences. Once again, our reaction may be of pleasure or displeasure.

So far, so good. What then of imagination? What is it?

Patanjali's description of this subtle concept is beautiful. He says that the *usage of words that are not based on actual knowledge* triggers imagination, which in turn is a kind of mental modification.

For example, you say of your friend, "She has a great imagination." Why might you have said so? Did your friend describe a green sky? Did she describe a moon made of fire?

We know these statements to be false and a product of your friend's imagination. The "mental modification", where your mind responds, has been caused by a falsehood. Once again, observe that your mind may find pleasure or displeasure in the modification, depending on what was communicated. Perhaps the image of a light green sky made you smile. Perhaps a moon on fire made you uncomfortable.

Imagination is induced by words that are not based on actual knowledge.

Patanjali moves to the fourth kind of mental modification, deep sleep. There is no tangible content per se, but the mind still swirls out of your control. You remember a small number of your apparently illogical dreams, spontaneously born in your sleep. They may be pleasant or unpleasant (like a nightmare), but they left an impact on your mind, didn't they?

Sleep may trigger dreams, which in turn stir the mind.

Here is an extract from a short story I once wrote involving the baffling illogic of dreams:

> I have watched myself go to sleep.
>
> Several times. Hovering about a foot above my body, I have watched the last twitches of my tired body, longing for an escape from reality—sleep. I have restlessly shifted from side to side, adjusting the bed sheets around me, sometimes on my back, sometimes on my side, and often on my stomach. I have watched myself clutch the pillow and adjust my head till the feeling was just right.
>
> Then I have welcomed myself into this other reality. I am never surprised to see myself again, unfailingly. It could almost be considered peculiar to hold my own hand and walk with myself into that space of illogic. But when we dream, we let completely random images, situations and consequences waft in from unexpected directions and are never caught off guard. We are never baffled.

Finally, Patanjali says that memory also affects the mind. As opposed to dreams, which seem to be spontaneously created and apparently lack an underlying logic, memory is based on the retention of experiences. Was it the perfume of someone with you in an elevator 30 years ago? Was it the sensation of satin on your skin many years ago? Perhaps the sharp features of a beggar at a railway station you saw 20 years ago? Some things *happened*, and the mind retained that experience; the mind was *modified*.

Were you able to be indifferent? No. Some memories are pleasant, and some make you comfortable. Others are acutely troublesome, and you wish you could forget them. Was it perhaps an act you committed or witnessed?

You may say, "Such and such an event is behind me. There is no need to be disturbed by it now." That is a noble goal but not easy to attain. Our passions are stirred by recalling or experiencing something or dreaming about it.

Memories based on facts also affect your mind.

Patanjali then makes a clear and firm statement:

With sincere practice and dispassion, you can control and eliminate all these sources of fluctuations!

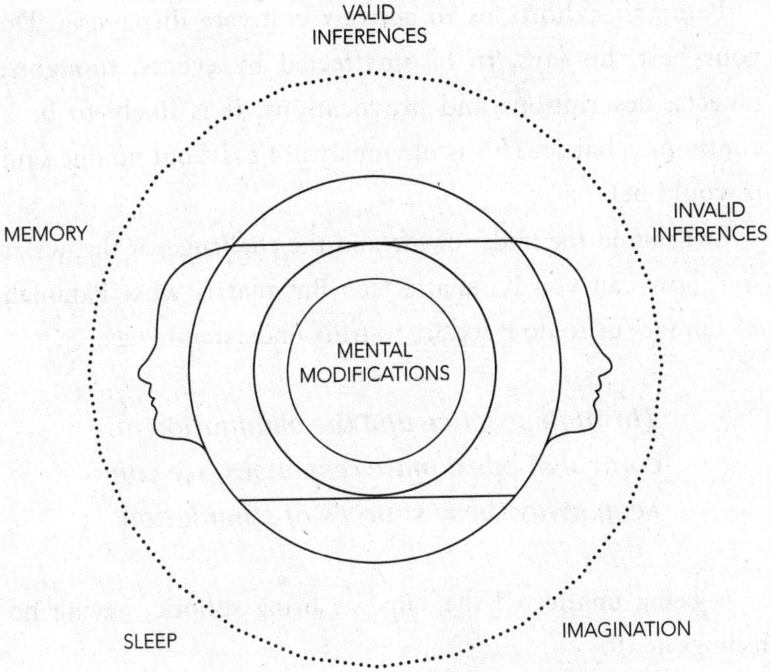

Patanjali continues his beautiful commentary, dissecting the subtlest and gravest of concepts. He explains the phenomenon of dispassion, needed to still one's mind.

Dispassion is a complex word. When you are impacted by all those feelings and emotions which apparently define being human, how can you afford to treat all these assaults on your mind without reacting?

If nothing else, you could consciously develop a certain measured distance between you and whatever the world throws at you. Did someone praise you? Did someone criticise you? Can you try to have the same response to both by acknowledging but not reacting? That is dispassion.

Patanjali exhorts us to actively cultivate dispassion. Do your best, he says, to be unaffected by events, thoughts, objects, descriptions and provocations. It is likely to be a continuous battle. This is obviously not easy, but no one said it would be!

Swirling in the midst of life and the challenges it throws at you, how can you be unaffected? But that is what Patanjali encourages us to do if we are to truly understand yoga.

Through practice and the elimination or control of passionate responses, we can keep away these sources of stimulation.

Is being unaffected the same as being robotic, having no feelings at all?

Not really. Compassion also needs to be present. Otherwise, this kind of dispassion implies indifference to the principle of dharma (duty) and the suffering of other living beings.

To make sure we understand, he explains why practice is so critically important. Whether you practise the violin or practise painting or dancing, or anything else, you know this: relentless effort propels you to perfection.

Even in this (the effort to still fluctuations), determined, continuous practice is an absolute must!

Patanjali moves to the next, even more beautiful level. He says that indifference to the results of knowledge or the evidence of nature is the highest form of dispassion. Nothing should be desired; nothing should cause feelings of pride (possessing knowledge, for instance). For example, if you know a subject—

say music—relatively well, there is a possibility that you feel a sense of pride that you know something that others do not. Can you keep that feeling of pride away?

Indifference to the results of knowledge is the highest form of dispassion.

All this is very challenging and requires diligent, patient cultivation.

This point about indifference comes up often in subsequent chapters.

So, let us take a breather now.

We actually covered the first 14 sutras of the original Yoga Sutras!

In these, Patanjali builds a foundation for our understanding of achieving union with the Absolute, the Supreme. By confronting the turbulent mind, we may develop strategies for mastering it and continue our journey.

As I reflect on my own life, I see that I have had some minimal degree of success in controlling my mind, and many failures too. Limited success has come through the regular practice of the asanas and music because both require concentration and the blocking of extraneous thoughts.

But that alone has not been enough. These sutras provide exemplary understanding of the nature of the stormy mind and offer direction on how to deal with it.

In these 14 sutras of the Samadhi Pada, Patanjali says, in summary:

- To attain union with the Infinite Reality, you need to be able to cease the modifications of the mind.
- There are five kinds of modifications: valid inference, invalid inference, imagination, sleep and memory. These modifications are hindrances or obstacles in your journey.
- By determined practice, you can manage these modifications, develop dispassion and still the mind.

Sutras 15–29

Patanjali has thus far encouraged the stilling of all thought: identify the sources that cause the mind to respond, but do not respond. Because if you do, you are adding another layer that says, "I am involved with the process of living." This adds another delay to the journey towards your final goal.

Detachment from the act and sensation of living is necessary. Once this happens, the goal is within reach. Till then, distractions continue to create obstacles.

He now describes two categories of the final goal of yoga, or the union with the Infinite Reality. This goal is called samadhi.

In the first category of samadhi, which is referred to as *Samprajnata*, he speaks of four stages to be experienced before attaining the state.

- Absorption with physical awareness
- Absorption with subtle awareness
- Absorption with bliss
- Absorption with one's true identity

These are mentioned several times in his text, but for now, Patanjali, as a guide, mentions the stages for you to take note of. Let us take a moment to understand them briefly.

1. In the first stage, we focus on an object. Let us take that object to be a tree. Then, we focus on the tree and block

out everything else.

2. In the second, we become absorbed in the object. In this stage, we imagine ourselves to be part of the tree. We lose our sense of being different from the tree.

3. In the third, we become internally absorbed by the elements that create thoughts. We now step back from the tree and examine the sensory objects that create the thoughts. Was it the eyes that witnessed something, perhaps the green leaves, and termed it "pleasant"? Was it an "odour" that the nose translated to "unpleasant"?

4. In the fourth, we transcend even these elements of cognition and reach the realms of our true nature.

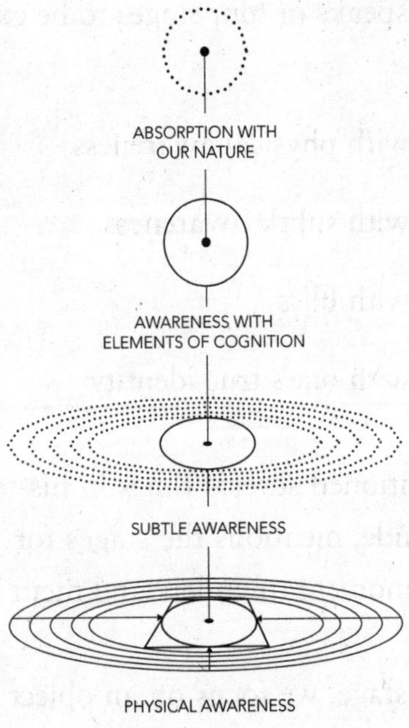

Here is another example to illustrate the concept.

- I touch the violin and think about the music I wish to produce.
- Next: my fingers move on the violin as an extension to thoughts formed in my brain and create the music. I am a part of the violin.
- Next: I have heightened awareness of the music itself, and the violin, external to me, loses its relevance.
- Next: I am now consumed by the thoughts and feelings that the music invokes.

What is the purpose of all this?

As mentioned earlier, the idea is to control and eliminate the sensory perceptions that result in assaulting and distracting the mind. When sensory pleasures are controlled, reduced and eliminated, samadhi is reached.

This requires significant effort. But unless you try, you will never know. Try to block out the temptations that the sensory organs present to you and that which the mind craves. It is hard, very hard. But it can be done with practice.

But other than the stagewise process of achieving samadhi, Patanjali says that there is another way, which he calls *Asamprajnata*.

This method involves a forceful, determined extinction of all thought. This is a peculiar notion—a thought to eliminate all further thoughts. Can we liken it to the last flicker of a flame before it is extinguished? Or a drop of water in the last stage of evaporation?

This involves personal discipline of the highest magnitude. The previous method, samprajnata, at least offers a four-stage path; Asamprajnata is a long jump, metaphorically speaking.

As you might now feel, Patanjali is now going into significant depth, addressing the mind's quixotic nature! Recognising the vaporous mind as the biggest impediment to attaining yoga, he provides guidelines to extinguish it (the mind's fluctuations) by a gradual process of eliminating sensory distractions.

Is there a state of existence between the physical and the formless?

Patanjali asserts that there is a state of disembodiment that some are in after leaving the physical body. They have no physical identity but are collections of formless intelligence. They have indeed transcended thought and engagement with sensory stimulation but still retain some past experiences, called samskaras in Sanskrit, or strong impressions of past experiences.

During the course of our lives, we may encounter persons who comment that the reason some other person was blessed or cursed was possibly because of his past *samskaras*.

Patanjali links this to the last kind of samadhi mentioned, asamprajnata.

The assertion here is that the forceful attainment of samadhi leaves behind residues, which linger on as amorphous intelligence, retaining impressions of the mind.

Incidentally, this observation has been the subject of a lot of debate. A brilliant commentator on the Yoga Sutras, Vachaspati Mishra, likens this idea to frogs who are activated during the rainy season but who otherwise are inactive!

And now Patanjali's words take on a hue of beauty! I found myself quite fascinated by the subtlety of his thoughts.

Certain preconditions exist before approaching asamprajnata, he says.

- Clear faith that samadhi is the goal.
- Strength and vigour, which we will cross-reference to the third limb of the eight folds of yoga, to be discussed in the next section on the Sadhana Pada. Patanjali's point is that it will not be possible to meditate for extended periods of time if your body is not in good condition and you have not mastered the ability to sit still in various yogic postures while breathing calmly.
- A stable mind, where fluctuations are controlled.

Patanjali encourages us by saying that anyone who works towards the goal with intensity—even if with varying degrees—will be successful. This is a recognition that not all can function or demonstrate commitment at the same level. Yet, sincerity will triumph.

This is the first time in his text that we see a direction that a healthy body is necessary!

Patanjali now introduces a matter of faith in the Almighty or the Supreme Entity. This theistic matter is unusual in the broader context of his text. However, it clarifies that another vehicle exists to obtain the goal of yoga if you believe in God.

In the given context, we may consider this entity to be the ideal person in all respects—timeless, all-powerful, all-knowing and limitless in all ways. It is this ideal that we aspire to be. This attitude of faith certainly softens our mind, making it receptive to knowledge!

How do we focus on this entity that seems impossible to comprehend? Chanting has been an age-old way that helps in concentration. The world over, repetitive chanting has been a way in which traditional cultures have tried to connect with a divine entity.

Can the chanting of a single syllable 'Om' help you? Indeed, it can, and it does, we learn, because it helps to develop the discipline of focusing. In our cultural traditions, bhajans and *dhrupad* music provide a similar directional argument that the repetition of sound is a sure way to keep distractions away.

I have had the good fortune of learning Indian classical music and writing about it. Here is something I once wrote about the morning Raag Lalit, touching upon Om:

Was this Raag not born from Om, the fundamental sound of existence? Yes, holy, divine and grave spirit, have You not promised that the sound of Om will take me to the heights of spiritual bliss?

Patanjali does a great service by not insisting that only prior recommendations apply. He provides a chain of logic as below:

1. You can obtain the goal of yoga through devotion to God, referred to in the text as Ishwara, the complete *Purusha*, or cosmic energy.→
2. Per Patanjali, Ishwara is a special entity, indifferent to obstacles of all kinds and therefore impervious to karma, karmic actions and their fruits.→
3. He is incomparably all-knowing.→
4. He is the greatest of teachers (guru) because he is not limited by time since he is neither created nor dies. →
5. Om ॐ is the sound in which Ishwara dwells. (This sound is also synonymously called *pranava*.)→
6. By repeating the sound of Om, you gain the ability to focus on Ishwara.→
7. This results in a complete understanding of the Self and an ability to be indifferent to all disturbances.

The recitation of the hypnotic syllable ॐ Om in the Indian cultural ethos starts making sense. I often wondered why people would say "Om Shanti" or "Hari Om", for instance. Now we see that chanting Om is a mechanism to focus and avoid distractions while proceeding to merge with the Supreme.

These, then, are the lessons from Sutras 15 to 29, all of which you can read in the original text at the end of this book:

- There are two types of samadhi, the end goal of yoga.
- There are four progressively intense stages in the first kind, with a focus on sensory withdrawal. The second kind is a determined "leap", which has a few preconditions.
- You may get the same results from chanting the syllable Om, which encapsulates Ishwara, defined as someone of timeless, unlimited power, embodying perfection.

What I learnt from Sutras 1 through 29 of the Samadhi Pada

Most of us have been, at some point in our lives, troubled and confused. We are unable to explain our reactions to events external to us. We cannot understand why we are alive and why we are attached to life. Why do we crave pleasure? Why is mental or physical pain so uncomfortable?

What does it all mean?

I, too, have been no different. My life has had its ups and downs. I have experienced pain and pleasure. I have lost relationships. I have often been overcome by a feeling of helplessness that I could not alter my circumstances meaningfully. All of us may have experienced this to varying degrees.

Like many others, I began my exploration of yoga by first addressing the physical dimension. It helped me feel more in control and gave me doses of enthusiasm and a sense of accomplishment. To be absolutely truthful, I had no real idea there was any other dimension.

I drifted along, with no clear purpose, preoccupied by the here and now, unclear about what to expect out of this experience called life.

The larger question of what the purpose of life was, was answered in the first few lines of the Yoga Sutras. I understood that observing my unruly mind and disciplining it was a good step.

If, for instance, someone spoke sharply to me, I separated three components:

- First, the source,
- Second, the message, and
- Third, how my mind was reacting or was expected to react.

Blocking out the first two is easy, with some effort. But the third is where the challenge lies.

By conducting this separation often enough in a conscious way, I have now been able to develop a modest capacity to prevent myself from reacting and adding fuel to the fire. No one wins in an emotional argument. By recognising this fact, I develop a buffer every time and disregard my mind's enthusiastic urging to respond.

Acknowledge. Do not react as far as possible.

This ability is not easy to acquire, of course. I cannot claim I have mastered it—and I do regress, allowing my mind to be altered by logic, falsehoods, imagination, dreams and memories, as warned by Patanjali. These alterations again cause reactions and emotional ferment.

But overall, despite occasional failures, I understood that the phrase "This too will pass" was an appropriate way to look at all the distractions that the mind was drawn towards. This was a major step in self-management for me, and in deriving a meaning for why I live at all.

In modern management parlance, a term called emotional intelligence (EI) is often used. The first stage of EI is to develop the capacity to notice the emotional state one is presently in.

The second stage is that of doing something about it.

For instance, I might acknowledge "I am angry." I might then say, "Let me do something about it."

This is good and healthy.

But a few lines of Patanjali's Yoga Sutras helped me go beyond with the suggestion that emotion itself ought to be tightly curbed and reduced. It is not easy.

On the personal front again, the issue of sound suddenly became highlighted through the reference to "Om."

My musical journeys have become more thoughtful. The audience is not important. Appreciation by others is not important. Sound serves as a vehicle for meditation and self-control.

I create the sound.

I am the sound.

2

Mastering the Distractions to Access the Rewards

Sutras 30–40

Patanjali has thus far created a vision for us.

Your life indeed has a purpose. It is for you to acknowledge that a state of tranquillity exists called samadhi. This state of perfect merging with the Infinite Reality, while keeping tight control over all the possible ways your mind craves flux and imbalance, is achievable using a few techniques.

None of these methods is easy, and they all require focus, discipline and dispassion. And a desire to get to the goal. Additionally, the vehicle of a simple resonating sound—Om—gives so much hope to a frantic mind.

So, there it is—a beautiful, extremely satisfying state to work towards to give meaning to our lives.

But I wondered if merely showing the end goal and

explaining the qualities you need to cultivate along the journey was enough. Had Patanjali spoken about distractions and other impediments?

I opened the book again and continued with the 30th sutra in the Samadhi Pada.

And right away, Patanjali speaks of a set of challenges.

The list you will see in a moment is a complete enumeration of the distractions you may encounter that keep you away from your goal. These are the human qualities that generate negativity, cloud your judgement and pull you along in the relentless current of worldly matters.

We are indeed encouraged to behave in these various unproductive ways by societal pressures; this brainwashing distorts our sense of values and diminishes what is truly and eternally beautiful.

I had no choice but to dwell on my own less-than-satisfactory experiences. At precisely the moments when I thought I saw glimmers of light and hope ahead, I would drive off the road.

Let me list all the things that were self-created potholes on the road to my yet-indistinct destination—samadhi:

- *Erratic health:* I experienced severe headaches that radiated beyond my head into the general well-being and happiness of my family, the composition of which expanded and contracted over the years. Malaria one week, stomach aches a little later, non-specific aches and pains—I lurched from one illness to the next. Were they truly physiological problems or a figment of my immature mind that manifested them?

- *Inertia:* I experienced erratic levels of energy that caused me to crave the escape of sleep, avoid social interactions one day and be extremely gregarious the next. I postponed decisions and avoided uncomfortable but necessary interactions, thereby compounding the problem, whatever it was.

- *Doubt:* I was plagued by endless self-doubt. I continued raging battles in my head, shouting angrily at myself. "Could I do a particular activity? No, that person there is more intelligent and more resourceful. I am ordinary and have never excelled."

  I went over all my shortcomings repeatedly in my head. I felt I redefined the word "failure".

- *Carelessness:* I practically cultivated absent-mindedness. I sometimes forgot where I was and what I was doing. I shaved twice a day. I forgot to eat. I searched for my glasses while wearing them. I lost items and was robbed because of not exercising due care. I created messes and became one.

- *Laziness:* I pretended I was a creative genius and was entitled to while away time. Whatever needed to be done immediately, I decided to do "later". Why study now? Why not later? Why fill out that form now? It could certainly be done in two minutes, just before it needed to be submitted. Why not sleep right away instead of a couple of hours later? Why iron my clothes? They would get messed up again soon anyway, wouldn't they? I developed sophisticated treatises for doing nothing.

- *Desires:* I was consumed by sudden and extreme obsessions with people, either liking them excessively or hating them beyond reason. I took an inordinate interest in certain types of food because I loved the taste. I craved music from a particular musician. I was a slave to my senses and thought it was a good thing and what made me human.
- *Delusions:* I had a great opinion of myself. I imagined that the entire world was enacting a complex drama just for me. I spent prolonged periods of time building castles in the air, imagining that I was a god-like creature sent down as the last answer to mankind's problems. How vain!
- *Endless restlessness and an inability to focus:* I lacked firmness in purpose and decisiveness. I struggled through periods of being bored quickly. Classes were boring, tasks were dull, jobs were tedious. The moment I attained something, it lost its meaning and value. I read a book and put it aside after reading two or three pages. Nothing made sense.

Illness, delusion, laziness, instability, weakness, cravings, lack of confidence and focus are our distractions on our way to our final goal.

In a single line, Patanjali maps out all the issues and problems that every person will face and must consciously overcome. These are precisely the experiences I have had, which embedded me deeper and deeper in problematic human experiences.

You cannot come up with solutions unless you know what the problems are!

You could argue—and you could be right—that the challenge of attaining a desirable state of tranquillity while still existing in the turmoil of everyday life is extremely difficult, almost absurd. It may even detract from the very experience of living!

Yet, if we were to step away from each of the diminishing experiences listed above, we may realise the beauty of yoga.

In other words, cultivate good health. Catch yourself being lazy and correct yourself. Work on your self-confidence. Avoid fantasies—the product of imagination, which we spoke of in the previous chapter. Observe the growth of desire and reduce it consciously. Observe thoughts and actions that indicate instability and dampen them.

All these are ultimately hurdles and distractions on the journey.

What happens when you allow yourself to be distracted by illness, poor behavioural patterns, desires and delusions?

Your breathing becomes rapid and shallow. Anxiety sweeps your awareness, your pupils dilate, you despair for the solution that makes sense to you. The impact on your physical being is negative, while your mind ferments due to distractions. And your heartbeat goes up!

The first sign of an unquiet mind is shallow breathing.

The quiet mind watches these perturbations and gently sweeps them aside, craving the stillness of a remote lake.

Patanjali recommends something simple: strive for a state of focused awareness.

Meditate.

Cultivate the art of meditation.

Like everyone else, I always thought of meditation as something I could not do. It seemed pretentious, wholly impractical and a cowardly way to escape reality.

Assuming you do see—however reluctantly—a value in meditation, you may experience, over time, a certain peace that is hard to describe fully. Suffice to say that all the human experiences that caused so much stress will suddenly seem small and insignificant. As your mind recognises this and declines to engage with negativity, the body responds too.

In my own case, I have observed that my heartbeat can reduce to about 55 beats per minute from the regular 73. This involves deep breathing and a complete focus on the movement of breath and a determined blocking out of all sensory distractions.

But the question that needs to be asked is—meditate on what?

Patanjali approaches this matter with a deceptively simple exhortation: *Meditate on a single object.*

But before beginning the practice of meditation, the cultivation of positive traits is essential. Our obsession with negative and distracting influences can reduce by shifting our focus to the opposite set of traits.

Patanjali urges us to develop qualities like friendliness, compassion and joy. These are not distractions because these sentiments are directed towards those who are happy, unhappy and virtuous, respectively. And for those who are caught in the web of wickedness and anger, be indifferent. They have to go through their journey alone. It is their karma.

How remarkable!

I remember harbouring routine sentiments of jealousy towards those who I perceived were more successful or somehow different in a "better" way.

I allowed myself to be obsessed by my health and created ailments where none existed.

I was irritated by those who seemed pointlessly happy. I avoided those I felt were chronically unhappy.

And I allowed hostile and crooked individuals to control me by making me react to their negative actions.

All these were nothing but self-created minefields (or *mind fields*!).

Does all this sound familiar? Are we all guilty of little acts of self-sabotage?

Once you recognise these bubbles of distraction, you can do something about them.

And through meditation, you attain a state where breathing becomes slow and steady, your brow clears, and your mind settles and sinks deep within. The focus of your mind shifts to the very act of breathing.

Perfectly timed, acutely conscious exhalation starts resembling the removal of distractions.

Suspending breathing for short periods after exhalation or

inhalation leads to a grounding of oneself.

Put together, the mind settles into a rhythm and attains the state of a remote, still lake.

Many years ago, I wrote a book on classical music. Here is an extract from it that makes the same point:

> How beautiful the focused, calm mind is. No thought dares disturb the mind that has found peace through singing me. The eternal truths are twined within every phrase you make and create within me, and they do not see the need to hide or be elusive.
>
> Why be reborn? You can commit no evil when you sing me. Your sins melt and drip away as you go past Nishad and into the next octave, exploring, exploring, asking the same questions over and over and waiting to listen to the answers again and again because they are so clear. Your mind will dive deeper and deeper into the depths of your soul, finding more and more and yet returning effortlessly to the present, understanding that the restlessness of the outer world is an illusion that must be endured till your soul is ready to move on from its temporary home.
>
> Your body does not seek your attention any more. Your mind becomes the incense for the outside world.
>
> After singing me, listen to silence and see that there was no difference after all.

Meditation is not that simple in practice, of course. Constant, unwanted thoughts come up abruptly, and you engage with them. You try to pull away from them and repeatedly fail. This is the single biggest reason people find meditation difficult and exasperating.

But those who recognise that this phenomenon is natural and stay the course are rewarded. Being able to amplify, isolate and eliminate sensory distractions through practice causes the mind to gain confidence.

The question of what one should meditate upon is important. And yet it may not be in the way you might think.

As all distractions wilt or are pushed away, a peaceful but determined focus on an object moves the mind inwards, deeper and deeper. And there, there may be a kind of light or awareness that you recognise, which is entirely impervious to distracting emotions.

I personally choose to meditate on a single note of music. I can focus on it, and soon I feel I am that note. That is not an exaggeration. The note then starts vibrating with meaning, making everything else seem quite inconsequential.

As our ability and confidence to meditate increases with time and practice, we see that we may no longer need a specific object to meditate on.

You may meditate on an external person who you judge to be an enlightened soul. Or you may consider the evanescent and unusual knowledge that emerges from sleep. Or you may meditate on absolutely anything once you have reached an elevated level of meditative control.

Apart from dwelling on a single note, I also use a technique that invariably gives results.

While deliberately controlling your inhalation and exhalation, slowing it down as far as possible, imagine yourself at the core of an expanding globe that zooms out from your body to the far reaches of the universe.

You may imagine yourself to be the infinitely large universe, which therefore reduces all activities and actions to meaninglessness, to immeasurably small blips.

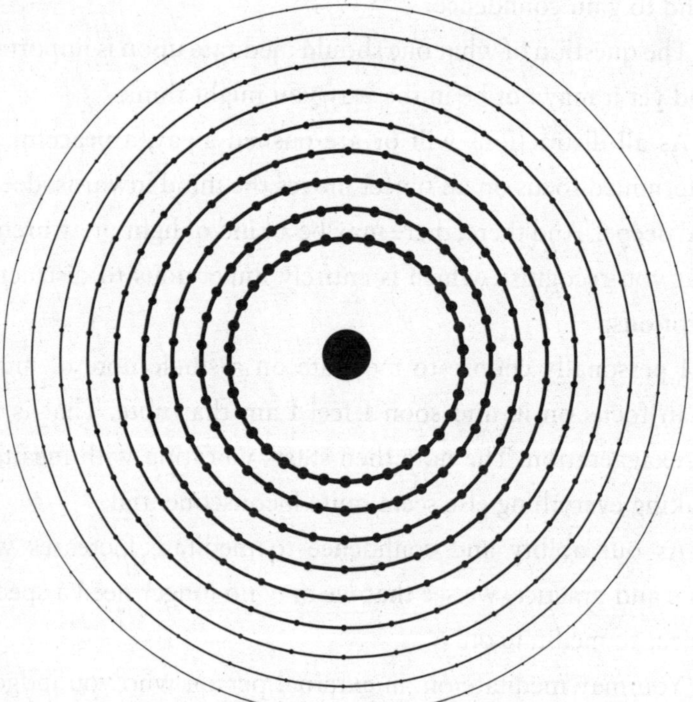

Or you can reduce yourself to a single, lone atom. In this case, the sheer expanse of space and time surrounding you similarly makes all activities a constantly swirling mass of chaos, which you observe but do not engage with.

Emerging from such an exercise gives you a halo of peace that must be experienced.

Indeed, as you will read later, Patanjali suggests that a true yogi transcends the immeasurably small to the infinitely large, all through the development of meditative abilities.

That is a deeply moving concept. The meditator crystallises all activity across the spectrum to fundamentally nothing.

The entire cosmos lies within the one who meditates.

These then are the lessons I gleaned from Sutras 30 through 40:

- The road to samadhi has multiple distractions–poor health, jealousy, laziness, self-doubt, delusion, lack of purpose, indiscipline and imbalance. This manifests in shallow breathing, a nervous disposition and negativity, like sorrow.
- Meditation is the answer but for that, you must first cultivate the right positive attitudes towards others and indifference to the negative and malicious.
- As meditative abilities increase, you can shift from focusing on an external object to the light within, and to anything at all, while spanning the cosmos.

Sutras 41–51

Patanjali's systematic and deliberate elaboration of the road to samadhi is at once satisfying and awe-inspiring.

It is an extraordinary observation: that a mind that soaks in all manner of disturbances under various guises is a mind that will never actually find peace and purpose.

And while the extremely subtle state of samadhi is described, as are the possible ways in which you can get to the final goal, the challenges that spring up and distract us from getting there are also laid out. Thereafter, recommendations are also provided.

Cultivating the practice of meditation is recommended as the means to gradually control your mind. This requires diligent practice and perseverance, initially taking some assistance from an external object to meditate on. As the practice becomes stable and confident, you may choose other objects to meditate on, including your own inner light. In this heightened meditative state, your mind masters size, space and time.

Having done so, I wondered what the mind in samadhi looks like. The ability to ignore all perturbations through a deliberate process of meditation while conquering all the impediments that crop up to entice your mind away—that is tough, to say the least! But after relentlessly and progressively surmounting challenges and reaching a state called samadhi, what does the destination look like?

Let us draw an analogy. Let us say you want to learn the guitar. That is your dream—you want to be a professional guitarist as you believe you have a gift for music. How would it work?

- First, fix the goal.
- Second, find a teacher to give you a method, or methods, to get to your destination.
- Third, practise, practise, practise. Never skipping a day. Avoid the temptation of postponing practice on some pretext or the other. Stay healthy and avoid distractions.

When you reach the final state of perfection, when you indeed become a professional guitarist, you will know that you cannot slip. The state of perfection is attainable but elusive at the same time. You will know when you hit a note perfectly, and you will also know that the same note will be shaky if you have not practised for even a day.

And then, there will be subtle variations in the very same note. Changes in volume, sharpness and resonance. These are the abilities of an expert guitarist. If we peep into the mind of a near-perfect guitarist, we might hear him say:

- I play a note on my guitar, wishing it to come forth in a particular way.
- That note comes forth exactly as intended because of relentless practice and discipline. I am now one with the note.
- It is heard by others precisely as it was produced. The audience does not hear any distortion. The listener is now one with the note and merges with it in his mind.

Patanjali beautifully describes the mind that has reached the state of perfection after mastering the ability to keep away from distractions while keeping at bay all those human frailties like laziness, poor health and so on.

This perfect diamond reflects everything and is everything. There is a beautiful convergence of three things: the perceived, the perceiver and the perception. There is no distinction.

That is the state of samadhi.

The perfect mind is like a diamond and reflects everything without distortion.

Is there only one kind of samadhi?

The unpeeling of the onion continues.

Samadhi of the first type—called *savitarka*, or "with the application of thought"—is achieved by imprints of words, ideas and names. Therefore, there are mild traces that swirl within, making the samadhi slightly less than perfect.

A previous commentator, Sankara, has helped progressively shape a clear understanding of how to understand or perceive this. He takes the example of how a cow presents itself in different ways to us. Let me paraphrase.

- *I see a cow named Lakshmi.* It is a specific cow that has a name.
- *I see a cow eating peacefully in a meadow.* The cow is seen

as an object, not easily distinguishable from many others grazing nearby. We do not know its name or if it has one.

- *I know that a cow is a gentle and harmless herbivore.* The cow is understood as an idea or concept in one's mind.

The mind in this kind of samadhi does dwell on such imprints, even if notionally and neutrally. This happens when the process of meditation uses these ways to achieve the purpose. Samadhi is achieved but with the help of external impressions, no matter how light. A tiny distortion remains. A seed remains.

This ability of extremely subtle perception is called *samapatti,* a word sometimes used interchangeably with samadhi.

But when the mind no longer needs the help of external impressions to achieve the state of samadhi, and it only needs your sense of self, your inner light, then we achieve the highest form of samadhi—*Nirvitarka*, or "without the application of thought". "Nir" translates to "without".

Now there is no distortion. We have now merged with the cow, in a manner of speaking. There is no residue or seed seen.

From my own perspective of looking at music, there is indeed a process of sinking deeper and deeper into a bottomless lake.

At the fringes of the lake of music, we think of the musician, the name of the raag and the composition, and what is intended to be conveyed. We enjoy the music and are in a state of bliss, akin to savitarka samadhi.

We can still feel the shallow depths of the lake with our feet, which are the traces of our knowledge of who the musician is, the intent of the composition and so on.

As we move slowly to the centre of the lake of music, sinking in its abstract beauty, we no longer need the musician or any other labels. We feel the inexpressible sentiment of the raag at the very core of our being and are lost in its self-generated vibrations.

Our feet no longer touch the bottom of the lake, and we willingly submerge in a bottomless lake of pure sound. The musician, composer and idea have disappeared from our peripheral consideration.

This is akin to nirvitarka samadhi.

Patanjali's models are quite remarkable. We have been taught that atoms are the smallest units of matter. Yet, Patanjali takes that even further and speaks of consciousness as the subtlest form of nature, which we call *prakriti*. And when you think about it, you see a pearl of deep, profound wisdom in what he says. We are aware. We are conscious. This consciousness, too, is a component of nature.

The most subtle form of nature is consciousness.

Once even this consciousness disappears into nature through continued meditation, it becomes a final expression of purity, with no further dissolution possible.

We are reminded that the savitarka samadhi achieved through imprints (samskaras) does not liberate you—yet—from the cycle of life and death. If residues remain while in the state of samadhi, we still fall short.

The possibility of karmic residues may exist. In other words, the karma accumulated in the lifetime of the yogi does remain. You will read more about this in a subsequent chapter.

Patanjali proclaims that attaining nirvitarka samadhi is the most desirable state. There is no connection, however tenuous, with the external world in any manner and no association with time and space. A light is formed within, and the mind radiates perfectly in all directions, unfettered in any way. This samadhi requires no logic, inference or testimony, and a final Truth is revealed.

This Truth, bereft of any seeded impressions (samskaras), brings with it freedom from the cycle of birth and death.

When this inner light, too, is finally extinguished, where there is absolute indifference to even wisdom, knowledge and the power of discrimination become entirely irrelevant, having no purpose, a final state of samadhi is reached.

We have sunk deeper and deeper into an indescribable sea of pure Truth and have finally dissolved in it.

What a seemingly endless and beautiful journey of self-discovery! What an inspiring way to go deeper and deeper into oneself for liberation, beyond atoms, beyond consciousness, beyond any residue of self-identification, for a final merging with the Infinite Reality!

These then are the top three lessons I learned from Sutras 41 through 51:

- In samadhi, the perfect mind is like a diamond that reflects everything without distortion.
- The subtlest form of nature is consciousness.
- Savitarka samadhi retains imprints from external influences. Nirvitarka samadhi relies on an inner light and is perfect in the sense of being beyond knowledge, logic and inference. Thereafter, our mind dissolves in nature.

What I learnt from Sutras 30 through 51 of the Samadhi Pada

The Samadhi Pada described in elaborate detail what yoga is, what samadhi means, the challenges that will distract you on your way and several other finer nuances.

One stand-out statement avers that the quiet mind declines to respond to the disturbances thrown at it. By developing the skill of meditation, we perceive an inner light that can be meditated upon. External aids can be used to slowly strengthen the process of inward focus. In the ideal case, meditation no longer needs anything external because those then remain as imprints and serve to continue the process of birth and death.

In the final instance, once unaided meditation, absolutely pure, dwells on the inner light and understands the Truth that is beyond words, it may then choose to move one step further. Consciousness, the most subtle form of nature, merges with the Infinite Reality, and true samadhi is reached.

In my experience, when presented with an attractive goal, it is necessary to prepare before proceeding.

Preparation involves also factoring in obstacles that may come up, with or without warning. Some are external to us, and some are self-created.

There is nothing unique in what I have said. In one's professional life, this is part of the game. We plan, we design, we take up matters as a project. Then we execute the project.

In this set of sutras, Patanjali's 360-degree, spherical view of the way to achieve samadhi involves acknowledging that all the experiences we take as being routine to the experience of living are also speedbumps on the road.

I looked at my emotional and behavioural responses that were fundamentally degrading to my sense of self. They were unproductive and entirely reflexive, often expressed with little time to think and respond in a measured way. Bouts of laziness, periods of self-doubt and even illness may seem valid and unavoidable at that moment, but when looked at dispassionately from a distance, are all braking influences. Bouncing back from such episodes requires double the effort. I have resolved to take Sutra 30 to heart and resist the need to react impulsively, as described earlier.

Sutra 30: ***Disease, inertia, doubt, carelessness, laziness, sensuality, delusion, physical or mental lack of vigour and instability are the barriers that distract the mind.***

On the other hand, there is nothing to be gained by being dour and overly obsessed with oneself. Acts of kindness with no expectation of a reward, sharing the joy of others, expressing compassion to those in distress and developing an ability to be indifferent to those with acidic tongues who seem to possess an innate cruel streak— all turn out to be very fulfilling. They create a stronger shell that resists provocations designed to alter your mind and derail your journey.

This actively cultivated set of traits manifests in a straightforward way—my breathing is regular, even slow. So, am I a calm saint? No, let me not give myself so much credit;

that is not true. But what can be said is that I have longer periods of balance now than imbalance. I am aware of this fact.

Being a practitioner of asanas for several years now, I know well the benefits of meditation. It is not just a technique of staying calm and slowing down, though even that is quite a good thing too.

Prolonged meditation allows you to observe the activities surrounding you more neutrally, as though it were a movie playing out that required minimal responses from you. It allows you to take a pause before a possible reaction while recognising the futility or even absurdity of a response. When earlier I might have taken grim satisfaction in a terse and pointed response that "destroyed" the provocateur, now it seems far more rewarding to listen to the hurtful words of others and choose not to be hurt. Even if I were to succumb and respond, I catch myself in the middle of the enunciation, recognise the futility of it, regret it and distance myself from the stimulus. This is an implosion and a recognition of a light within that needs no external fuel.

In the same way, receiving praise or appreciation needs to be acknowledged with a smile; the pleasure experienced is transient at best and must not be craved for. It modifies the mind and creates a new distraction, even if pleasant. It is also good manners!

Musical experiments have become more personal. There is no longer a need to crave anyone's appreciation. A note produced in solitude seems richer and more pregnant with meaning than one played for the aesthetic enjoyment of others.

Will I achieve samadhi one day, in this lifetime or the next? That is difficult to say. Even hoping for it recognises the sense of ego. It is better to focus on meditation and dispassion, observing the breath as it provides fuel to consciousness. It is better to listen to the vibrations of a note from my violin as it expands in all directions and slowly fades away. After a while, I may no longer hear it because of the limitations of my ear. But it continues into distant space. Finally, it merges with space itself.

And so, I recognise this: I am everything.

And I am nothing.

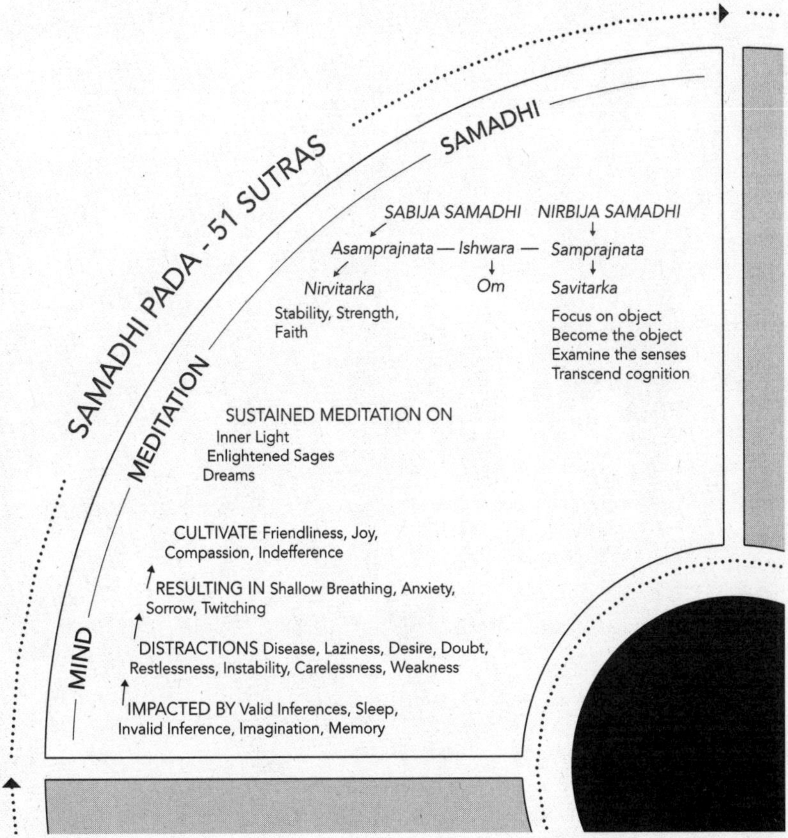
SAMADHI PADA - 51 SUTRAS
SAMADHI
SABIJA SAMADHI
NIRBIJA SAMADHI
Asamprajnata — Ishwara — Samprajnata
Nirvitarka
Om
Savitarka
Stability, Strength, Faith
Focus on object
Become the object
Examine the senses
Transcend cognition
MEDITATION
SUSTAINED MEDITATION ON
Inner Light
Enlightened Sages
Dreams
MIND
CULTIVATE Friendliness, Joy, Compassion, Indefference
RESULTING IN Shallow Breathing, Anxiety, Sorrow, Twitching
DISTRACTIONS Disease, Laziness, Desire, Doubt, Restlessness, Instability, Carelessness, Weakness
IMPACTED BY Valid Inferences, Sleep, Invalid Inference, Imagination, Memory

Section 2

The Discipline—Sadhana Pada

3

Tuning the Engine of the Mind

This then is the goal of life: to rise above the continuous provocations thrown at us disguised as pleasing and displeasing, to be cognisant of the fickle mind and its cravings, and work towards samadhi.

Yet, the mechanics of how to reach this state need greater understanding. You cannot read and write until you know the alphabet. Preparation is necessary for every sphere of life. And if samadhi is to be the highest endeavour of one's life, the nature of preparation needs to be known. Just wishing for samadhi is not enough.

While I felt I was ready to begin the journey, I was perplexed. How does one begin? Did I have the ability and qualifications? If not, how would I need to go about it? I seemed altogether too "human", not vastly different from any other, with strong likes and dislikes, unable to resist the beckoning of indulgences.

I could hardly sit still in meditation though I was improving very slowly. The only thing I was relatively skilled at was asanas, which I knew was just a small part of the solution. In fact, I was not even sure which part of the solution this would satisfactorily fit in.

I felt unconfident and incomplete.

Did Patanjali have something to say? I wondered.

He did.

Sutras 1–14

Patanjali's Sadhana Pada gives an elaborate description of the disciplines needed to work towards samadhi. This is where the references to the well-known practices of asana (postures) and pranayama (breath control) are seen.

He starts by saying that it is crucial to cultivate minimalism, similar to austerity, in one's meditation practice, study oneself objectively (with or without the aid of other spiritual texts) with great sincerity, and cultivate devotion and surrender to the formless and all-powerful entity who is the source of all creation, Ishwara, first referred to in the Samadhi Pada.

Minimalism, self-study and devotion are a prerequisite to approaching the disciplines needed to attain samadhi.

Minimalism (loosely synonymous with austerity) is a consequence of reducing all forms of comfort and sensory pleasures to practically nothing. It is the active cultivation of not allowing oneself to succumb to the cravings of the body. The mind seeks comfort in all things, drives our need for luxury and asks us to pamper the body. As we focus on what is profoundly important, austere meditation, which tests our resolve in all ways, becomes an important practice of purification. In the best case, we can actively live a simple life by reducing our needs to the bare minimum.

For instance, food is to be considered as merely a means

of nourishment and not a succumbing to the cravings of the tongue and the demands of the stomach. Similarly, do we really need five shirts when two shirts might do just as well?

Do we really need X? Do we really need Y? This question should pop up whenever we are considering acquiring something.

What is truly necessary? What is fundamentally unnecessary?

These are questions that Patanjali provoked. And as such, given that I had been hitherto doing quite the opposite, the matter became quite challenging.

There I was, building a career as a management consultant where I spoke of image management and dressing well. I wined and dined clients, spoke at elegant public settings and had a high-end car.

Not even one of these things was necessary except to massage my ego.

Now I was encouraged to suddenly swerve away and strive towards the opposite!

How difficult it is to be minimalistic when all the messages we get from the material world stress the wonders of comforts! Why do advertisements suggest that a particular car is the most luxurious? Or that buying such and such mattress will help you sleep very comfortably? These signals entice you away into the world of transient pleasure. By firmly refusing to succumb to these allures, we establish discipline and refocus on what is profoundly important.

The study of scriptures of various kinds tempers our minds and gives us crucial perspectives into ourselves that supplement the drive towards samadhi. It prepares us for the understanding and practice of disciplines that will be discussed soon.

Self-analysis is not simple. We may need an external framework to conduct a proper study of what we are all about and understand where our strengths and weaknesses are.

And surrendering to Ishwara has the effect of developing humility and opening the mind to the profound perspectives needed to fully understand samadhi.

Incidentally, all these are components of *Kriya yoga*, which emphasises surrender to the Absolute (present within us) through chants, prayers and such (kriya means action). A driving theme is that self-interest is minimised or even eliminated.

1. Minimalism/Austerity
2. Self-study and study of scriptures
3. Surrender to Ishwara

These practices serve to weaken or even eliminate various negative distractions (referred to as *kleshas* in a later section on the Sadhana Pada). And as Patanjali explains, these weakened distractions and obstacles are a necessary precondition to a successful practice of the disciplines needed to move forward towards samadhi.

A point of view is that kriya yoga is as effective in our quest for samadhi as the eight limbs of yoga that will be described a little later; it need not be a precondition per se.

Once these pointers registered, I had to admit that the life I was leading, while not necessarily ostentatious, was certainly filled with objects and experiences that were not helpful to any spiritual quest. I seemed to have drifted along in the current of illusion, feeling smug and successful, not needing humility (or so I thought).

Patanjali makes us confront the five fundamental sources of sorrow that constantly bombard the mind.

When these five sources are not fully understood by us and then eliminated, they generate karma—the law of cause and effect—which is described in greater detail later. They therefore guarantee additional rebirths to deal with the fruits of karma, if not eliminated in the lifetime when karma sprouts.

The five sources—negative distractions (also referred to as kleshas)—are:

- One: Ignorance, or lack of knowledge. In this context, it drives home the message that the soul is distinct from the body. And therefore, the experiences of the body are fundamentally meaningless. This alone energises the subsequent four.
- Two: Attachment—to people, objects and experiences.
- Three: Egoism, which has a profound sense of self. Me. I. Myself.
- Four: Aversion—to sources of potential discomfort.
- Five: An inordinate fear of death or clinging on to life.

Sources of sorrow (kleshas) that create karma: Ignorance, Egoism, Attachment, Aversion and Fear of death.

I plead guilty to having been taken in by all five of these kleshas.

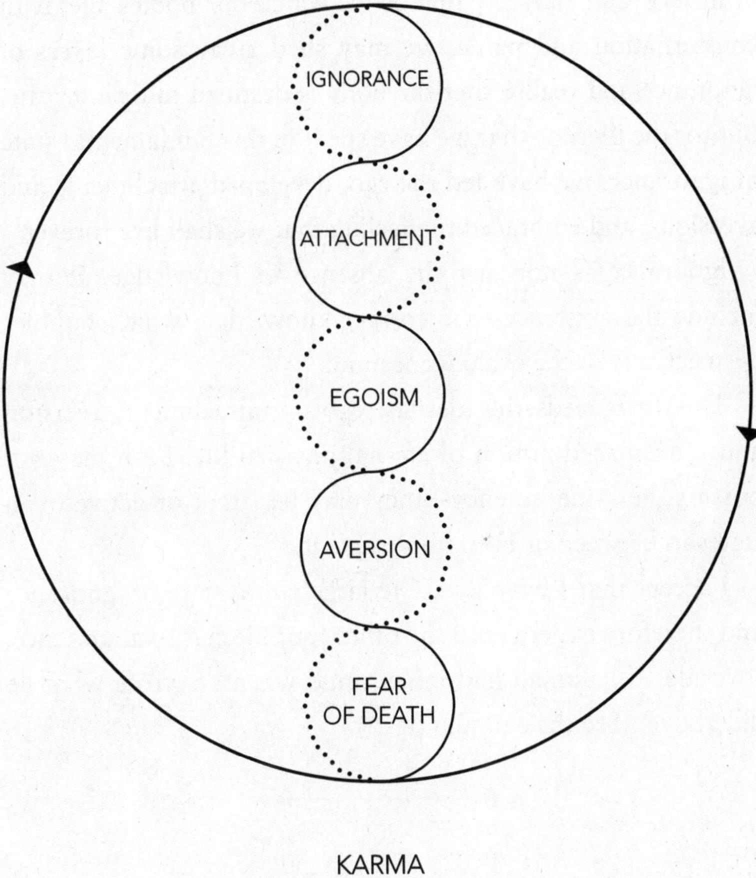

Our philosophical traditions teach us that life is only suffering. Even if we believe we are experiencing sensory pleasure, it will be followed very soon by separation and sorrow.

Patanjali proclaims that the soul is fundamentally happy, pure and eternal, while the body is precisely the opposite. If we are unable to differentiate between the two, then we are in a state of ignorance and will provide fuel to the other four sources of misery. One may say that as we watch our bodies age, with consternation and panic, we may shed away some layers of ignorance and realise that the body is destined to disintegrate. But for the lifetime that we have spent in this fundamental state of ignorance, we have fed the ego, developed attachments and aversions, and embraced the feeling that we shall live forever.

Ignorance is not just the absence of knowledge. It may include the existence of *incorrect* knowledge, which bubbles destructively in the evanescent mind.

This then feeds the kleshas: egoism, attachment, aversion and a misplaced notion of eternal physical life. Each may not possess the same potency—they may be latent or active or in states in between or even non-existent.

I accept that I have lived life largely in a state of ignorance and therefore experienced the other four kleshas in abundance. I wonder if Patanjali had me in mind when he wrote what he did above! (See the ego manifest!)

What then of the ego?

The subtlety of Patanjali's explanation is breathtaking and yet immediately obvious in the wisdom it contains.

I see, I perceive, I feel, I sense. I thus feel that this is truly the "real" me. But in fact, this is the ego throwing a veil of ignorance over the fact that the real "me" is separate from experiences. You are praised, you win awards, you receive recognition, you win an argument. In ignorance, you believe this—this illusion—is your true essence.

But indeed, it is not.

The ego is, therefore, a manifestation of ignorance.

When we transcend that and look forward to samadhi and the bliss of liberation that may be attained through it, we find the pleasures of life to be not only inordinately insignificant but also deceptive and pointless.

As ignorance feeds the ego, we then move to the endless quest for happiness. We are surrounded by messages suggesting that happiness involves buying something or loving someone, getting a huge salary, having a child or visiting Paris, and so on. And if we indeed do buy that object or acquire that illusory source of alleged happiness, we then hanker for more of the same. In other words, we become attached to the memory of that specific state of happiness and yearn for more experiences that feed that memory.

More power, more money, more property. It is a relentless cycle of deepening attachment, which triggers the drug of desire, and from there, even more corrupt notions of greed and anger, additional illusions of vanity and permanence, and finally, a degradation of core intelligence.

The attachment to a child, to a memory, to an object, to a career—all seem so necessary in the experience of life, perhaps because we have been led to believe it is the case, going back to the primordial need to survive, thrive and triumph. This transient happiness is never sated, and in its eternal quest, we continually fall short of the goal of samadhi.

And in an opposite manner, aversion points to a memory of an unpleasant experience, and we seek means to avoid it (the experience). If you dislike public speaking, if you dislike someone, if you dislike a subject, if you dislike conversing with your boss, these reactions are invariably due to past experiences that caused you discomfort. And not just in this lifetime! It could be a spillover from a previous one!

Once again, the ego seeks to avoid situations that show it in an uncomfortable light. We trace it back again to the belief that the ego deliberately separates the real self from the self that possesses a body and faculties of perception.

The ego separates the real self from the illusory self that perceives and reacts. When the ego is eliminated, the illusory world vanishes.

It is hardly surprising, therefore, that the idea of wishing to live in perpetuity is so attractive. Even though we see death around us, even as our family, friends and foes and complete strangers are finally consumed by death, we cling on to the belief that we are somehow different. The ego refuses to acknowledge that we too will die.

You see that in everyday life. Ask your friends and relatives if they have written a will. The vast majority will probably brush away the need to write one. They might even say that considering writing a will is inauspicious in some way! A nice and convenient mix of aversion and the fear of death!

The following story I wrote many years ago illustrates our constant battle with our ego.

The Destruction of His Ego

As the evening prayers at the monastery came to a close, the monks slowly opened their eyes to return to the present. The serene silence within spoke of great peace. The incense wafted across the large prayer hall and high up to the ceilings, calming the senses of the monks and the ordinary men and women who had come to meditate and find solace. Slowly, everyone dispersed without the slightest sound.

An old man, about 65, wearing nondescript clothes, stood up and walked across to where the Head Monk sat. He prostrated himself and sat with his thighs on his calves, resting on his knees and toes. He placed his hands on his knees, his eyes respectfully on the ground.

After five minutes, the Head Monk opened his eyes and spoke softly.

"Speak; what can we do for you?"

"I wish to suppress and destroy my ego completely," the man replied.

"I see," said the Head Monk.

After another five minutes, the man spoke.

"I have lived a full life. I have fame, power and money. I have children and grandchildren. I have a loving, devoted wife. I now wish to prepare for death."

"Have you known grief?"

"Perhaps much less than most people."

"Without experiencing grief, it is not possible to destroy your ego. Experience it, and then return."

The man withdrew respectfully.

He returned after several months.

"Well?" he was asked.

"Yes, I have experienced grief. My grandchildren died. And so did my wife."

"Anything else?"

"Yes, I lost my entire fortune."

"Very good."

"I seek knowledge and strength to cope with my losses."

After a long silence, the Head Monk said, "Your ego still exists. You are still worried about your own well-being. Work for the happiness of others without expecting to be observed and praised, without expecting recognition. Work in the darkness where you will not be seen performing good deeds."

The man withdrew respectfully. He gave away his clothes to the first beggar he met. He handed over his wallet to his driver and asked him to take away the car. He walked for several days to a faraway city where he was sure that no one would know him. There he worked in the slums, doing anything he possibly could to help anyone who needed it. He cleaned toilets, he slept on pavements, and he ate only if he was offered anything by anyone. He took unclaimed dead bodies to the crematorium and performed their last rites. He hugged dying dogs and comforted them till they died. He fed rats. He washed his body only when it rained. Disgust went away when he lived in filth. With disgust went away the fear of the unknown. Shame left him too. His own sorrow crept away from him as he attended to the miseries of others.

After several months, he returned to the monastery.

"Can I now conquer my ego?" he asked the Head Monk.

"The very fact you asked that question tells me you still have an ego and wish for something for yourself. Think about it and come back after six months," said the Head Monk.

The old man respectfully withdrew again and walked away slowly to a completely different town.

There, he continued doing what he had been doing earlier. He cut down on his needs even further. He ate next to nothing and even that, only at night, when no one was watching and could have no chance to feed him out of pity. He ate only if his eating would help someone else who sincerely wished to perform an act of piety. Whatever he found or was given, he gave away immediately and left before he could be thanked because that would have caressed his ego. When asked his name, he did not answer but turned and walked away. He stopped talking because words are an expression of the Self—either a longing or a question needing an answer or an opinion signifying individuality or a response indicating existence. He covered his eyes because to see would be to invite thought and comparison. He blocked his ears to prevent himself from responding or being swayed by laughter or cries of misery. He worshipped dogs and stones and prayed that the egos of others be erased. He no longer knew who he was.

At the end of six months, the monks waited for the old man to come to them for advice. No one came. After a few days, the monks conferred and arrived at a decision. They divined the location of the old man. Then they shut down the monastery and walked in a slow, silent procession to the city where he lived. They found him living in a filthy ditch surrounded by rats in the middle of a stinking, noisy, busy street.

He did not acknowledge the respectful greetings from the Head Monk. All the monks sat down in the muck on the road, and the Head Monk then prostrated himself at the feet of the old man. "Please teach us how to eliminate our egos."

In answer, the old man got up and walked away. To teach was to imply greater knowledge. Such awareness would revive his ego.

He was no longer interested.

Patanjali proclaims that even the wisest, who presumably are acutely aware that life is temporary, wish to cling to life.

Could this be because of the mental traces of past deaths that make us fear death?

Even the wisest cling to life because they are afraid of death.

Nevertheless, these five challenges or kleshas must be first weakened and then eliminated through the continuous practices that Patanjali prescribes.

The purest form of samadhi—asamprajnata—involves the mind dissolving into nature—prakriti—along with the debilitated seeds of sorrow.

It is logical then to consider that meditation is the prescription for managing these kleshas, which are potent sources of mind modifications. Elimination of the kleshas may additionally happen through the practice of kriya yoga.

Patanjali points out—and it seems acutely obvious now—that these five sources of sorrow create karma.

These five sources—ignorance, ego, aversion, desire and the fear of death—propel action that needs to be negated sooner—in the current lifetime—or later, in subsequent lifetimes. In this sense, we may see it as carrying forward the karmic account at death to subsequent births.

The sources of sorrow, rooted in ignorance, cause karma.

In summary, kleshas provoke and cause karmic fruition. At the time of birth, the accumulation of karma results in a determination of the following:

- One: the type of birth
- Two: the length of the lifetime, and
- Three: the proportion of pleasure and suffering to be experienced

We trace suffering back to ignorance, which radiates out to various kinds of delusions (ego, attachment, aversion and fear of death). This suffering comes disguised as pleasure. Karmic actions are generated when in the grip of delusion, which in turn manifests through ignorance, ego, attachment, aversion and the clinging to life because of the persistent, steadily escalating horror of approaching death. Attacking the roots of these sources is the only solution.

Sorrow arrives disguised as transient pleasure.

Such beautiful, deeply insightful observations from the radiant mind of Patanjali!

This then is what I absorbed from a study of the first 14 sutras of the Sadhana Pada:

- Austerity or minimalism, self-study and devotion prepare the mind for the actions needed in the quest of samadhi.

- The five sources of sorrow (kleshas) are ignorance, egoism, attachment, aversion and the fear of death. They create karma, which carries forward into additional births.

- These mind-altering kleshas can be weakened or eliminated through the practice of kriya yoga and meditation.

Sutras 15–28

The profound thoughts in the previous 14 sutras certainly had a major impact on me. The points are incisive; cultivated meditation is the only antidote for the five sources of ultimate sorrow. To root out ignorance, the mind and body need to be made receptive to additional streams of rigorous discipline.

As Patanjali continues in sutra 15, for the enlightened mind that witnesses the dance of life and has developed the acute sense of discrimination (referred to as viveka), everything reduces to suffering.

Suffering may be obvious in the sense that one experiences suffering as in physical pain or mental pain such as parting due to someone's death or other reasons. But it may also be the suffering caused due to the consequences of action or driven by your samskaras (the latent impressions spilling over from a previous birth).

And it may also be caused due to mind-modifications caused by the chaos of imbalance of the three subtle qualities that we possess, which are forever in a state of interdependent flux. These qualities are specified as:

- One: **Harmony**, in which one sees happiness and overall satisfaction, where intelligence is fully engaged. A person with such qualities predominating tends to be stable, calm and does not overindulge his senses.
- Two: **Activity**, by which repeated efforts are made to interact with the material world to maximise life

experiences. Passion, movement and a craving for the fruits of our action are the notable attributes of this subtle quality.

- Three: **Inertia,** through which everything is perceived as a dark and despondent place and activity is abhorred. A person with such enhanced qualities may tend to be lazy and generally negative in their outlook.

Naturally, a person is a complex, shifting mix of all three such qualities (otherwise referred to as gunas and identified as *sattva*, *rajas* and *tamas,* respectively).

Sattva, rajas and tamas are in a constant state of interdependent calibration.

For the one seeking enlightenment, harmony is sought by minimising activity and inertia as defined earlier. Nevertheless, all three remain in some (constantly changing) proportion, thereby guaranteeing that suffering due to craving is always around the corner.

When sattva predominates, there is a sense of pleasant euphoria, which seems temporarily satisfactory. The mind seeks challenges and attempts to be preoccupied by refined thoughts. This is the state the enlightened mind constantly strives for.

When rajas predominates, restlessness is visible. A man moves in the direction of illusory wants and seeks to satisfy himself in a variety of ways. It could be about seeking power, being excessively fidgety and action-oriented, and so on.

When tamas predominates, dullness, irritability and negativity manifest. There seems little reason to do anything. The mind is dark and wishes to be satisfied by existing material pleasure. Why bother with anything?

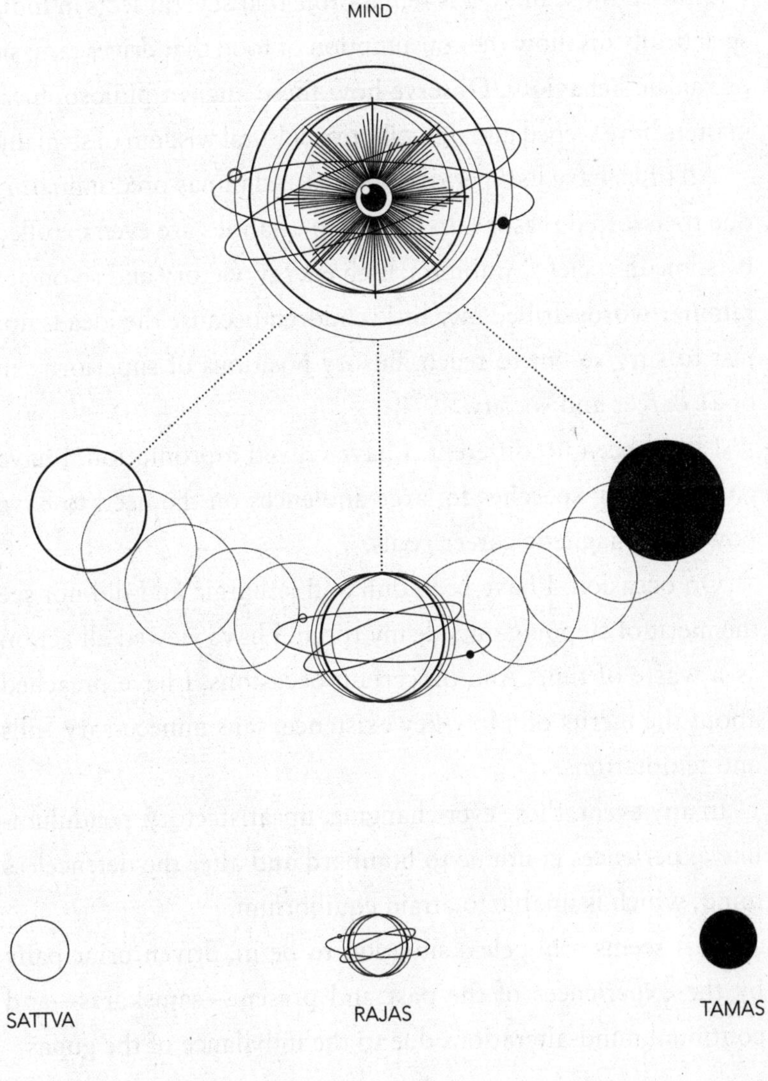

It is easy to understand why even the food you consume is labelled as sattvic, rajasic or tamasic because of the likely impact on the mind. Heavy food causes dullness. Spicy food may propel you into action. Bland food induces lightness and temporary bliss.

And on those lines, it is remarkable that several sects in India specifically disallow the consumption of food that drives tamasic or rajasic behaviour. Observe how these ancient philosophical matters have seeped into the collective cultural wisdom of so many.

All of us have had periods of rajas and tamas predominating due to assorted reasons. In fact, such qualities are even extolled by some in society. Ambition, high energy, victory and so on are familiar words drilled into little children because the idea is not just to survive but to reach illusory positions of superiority in one's career and society.

I have been no different. I have craved a promotion. I have given rousing speeches to large audiences on the need to have powerful, magnetic career goals.

On occasion, I have been dull and lethargic and did not see the merit of stepping outside my room. I have viewed all action as a waste of time. And on certain occasions, I have preached about the merits of a low-key existence, sans unnecessary frills and temptations.

In any event, these ever-changing, unsatisfactory, pendulum-like experiences continue to bombard and alter the defenceless mind, which is unable to attain equilibrium.

This seems a hopeless situation to be in, driven principally by the experiences of the past and present—samskaras—and continual mind-alterations due to the imbalance of the gunas.

The only thing we can control is the future. We can work out how to avoid suffering.

We can do little about past and present turmoil that pushes our behaviour in certain directions. But we can prevent actions that sabotage our spiritual quest.

And this is possible by (intelligently) understanding the world we interact with, which we see, is no more than figments of experience for the seer.

I see. My senses experience the seen, and my intelligence, just a layer over my true self, attributes qualities to it. I consume these experiences, as it were, and mistake my true self for that which experiences the outer world.

Patanjali then describes, in blinding clarity, the logic of why an external world exists at all.

The senses see the external world through the interplay of the three gunas. The seen exists for either of two purposes:

- One: for one of acute discrimination (possessing viveka), as a means of liberation.
- Two: to continue the experience, which entails the instinctive love of pleasure (which leads to sorrow, as mentioned) and an abhorrence of pain or discomfort.

Unless this "experience" is noted for what it is, an illusion, the first purpose will not be achieved.

You will endure rebirth repeatedly.

Patanjali, in the 18th sutra, lays out a detailed and fascinating exposition of how the gunas receive sustenance. Why do these three qualities of the human psyche behave in the way they do?

Paraphrasing from Edwin Bryant's remarkable commentary on the Yoga Sutras:

> "The five elements that absorb knowledge: ears, eyes, skin, tongue and nose—and the five organs that connote action (the tongue, hands, feet and the excretory and reproductive organs)—and the responsive mind—are the manifestations of the ego, and continuously work on the mind that is yet unable to discriminate between what is real and what is not."

Put together, we see that the forces that continuously juggle the gunas refuse to distinguish between the seer (pure, unchanging consciousness) and the seen (always changing and temporary).

The seer witnesses the fluctuating mind as it responds to stimuli through the layer of intelligence.

The seen exists only for the sake of the seer.

This is a very profound statement.

By itself, that which is seen is not aware of itself.

Pain does not know pain. Pleasure does not know pleasure. The experience is that of the seer, who must learn to dissolve the seen.

And to repeat in a separate way what was stated earlier:

- For the liberated, the seen disappears.
- For the non-liberated, the seen persists.

Isn't that beautiful?

We then refer to the possibility of a multiplicity of the seers (referred to as *purushas*), some who no longer engage with the previously seen, knowing it is illusory and others (non-liberated purushas) who continue to believe in the distinction.

Patanjali expands on the nature of the relationship between the seer and the seen. Purusha, pure consciousness, possesses the external world, prakriti, in all its dimensions.

Prakriti is unmasked as being nothing but a facilitating instrument for purusha. Till the state of discernment is not reached, we exist in a state of ignorance, further feeding the other gunas. That ignorance is also rooted in samskaras—latent impressions of existence. And yet, as was discussed in the Samadhi Pada, true liberation happens when intelligence ceases to function once ignorance is erased.

And that is how the seer is truly freed!

The ability to erode ignorance needs time to hone. A lot of time. It requires deep focus and constant rejuvenation. It needs the competence to finely discriminate (viveka) nuances of the integrity of knowledge. This ability improves as one whittles further down, always choosing a finer path when presented with choices. But sustained efforts are necessary to distinguish between what is real and what is not.

At this point, Patanjali says that this relentlessly cultivated ability to discriminate brings us closer to true knowledge (samadhi) in its purest form. It is seen in seven (progressive) steps. Specifically, integration with the body, the senses, life energy, the mind, the intellect, consciousness and the soul.

Through sincere dedication to the practice of these seven steps of yoga, each of which serves a critical purpose, spiritual illumination is reached, which transcends bookish knowledge or the words of scholars.

These are the lessons I gleaned from sutras 15 through 28 of the Sadhana Pada:

- The three gunas of sattva, rajas and tamas are in constant flux and act in concert. They ensure the continuance of suffering.

- The "seen" exists solely for the "seer" to recognise his own true nature.

- Spiritual enlightenment is achieved through the unceasing pursuit of discrimination to isolate and erase ignorance.

What I learnt from Sutras 1 through 28 of the Sadhana Pada

Cathartic experiences are often difficult to verbalise and even more difficult to write about.

The mix of blinding logic and philosophical insights in the cumulative reading from the Samadhi and Sadhana Padas till sutra 28 certainly threw me into a state of pleasant confusion. I was glad that I was able to grasp the significance of several points to a modest extent.

I thought about what I had read. In retrospect, how much had I been driven by illusion? To what extent had I recognised illusion for what it was and refused to engage with it?

In preparing for the journey of samadhi, there were a few awkward gaps: I have hardly been oriented towards the good practice of bowing to Ishwara in whatever form, though I have not been indifferent either. Does the fact that I seem to want less and less of practically anything material seem like a good thing? And yet, because of my life experiences and accumulations, I seem to have inordinately more than what I truly need, and certainly more than most others who seem to want what I have. So how do I get rid of things and actively seek a simple life free of fringe comforts? Could I truly claim to be tilting towards minimalism?

Perhaps, yes—in some matters, though not all. This will be a work-in-progress. I am embarrassed by the rather fancy yoga mat I recently acquired—this is true dissonance!

And then, continuing, have I studied myself enough to help

me develop the right frame of mind, as Patanjali had advised? Perhaps not as much as I could have. Have I studied scriptures to make my self-analysis that much more objective?

On the other hand, merely studying the Yoga Sutras may be helpful, packed as they are with so much wisdom. Now I can examine myself critically and remove stubborn imperfections. It requires will and a willingness to remove the mental rust that has accumulated over the years and accept my flaws.

But, without a doubt, a new strand of reflective awareness has been introduced. I now see the complete set of my experiences as a continuous movie, and I am able, from time to time, to hold back from engaging with it. This ability needs time to become automatic, but it is there. I see an internal light—only a flicker, but nevertheless, at least an occasionally glowing ember.

I experience joy and know it will not last, and then I will hanker for more. And then I am perplexed—I may realise that the joy I experience will go. But should I not play with a small child and give her joy?

I experience pride and realise that my ego feeds on it. Even using the word "I" now causes thought—who indeed am I? Am I the person who responds angrily to what I perceive as unfair criticism? Or am I the person who, when once robbed at an ATM, was calm and peaceful during the experience, thinking all this was a dream and it didn't really matter eventually?

I am not fully able to grasp what death might mean. Will I live to be 60? 75? 90? I do see the signs of deterioration though I am quite healthy. But wait! In that corner of my room is a stack of assorted medicines and ayurvedic oils! Is it because I am obsessed with my body and keep trying to fix it in multiple ways, slowing the slide toward death?

Should it matter at all?

Who then sees and experiences? What kinds of discernments am I capable of applying in my decisions? I fail and rise repeatedly. I see a situation as transient, something for which a response is not necessary. But some other situation brings out a response from me—say injustice to an animal. Anger bursts out. If I do not engage with this experience, would the suffering of another sentient being not be prolonged? What a conundrum!

What about the set of negative actions I might have taken over my lifetime? Could I blame it on a past accumulation of karma that forced my hand, whether impulsively or deliberately? Those actions may trigger another harvest of karmic fruits. But now, becoming more aware that the "seen" exists only to bring awareness to the "seer", it may be possible for me to exercise deliberation.

Yesterday, I was agitated by a message I received on WhatsApp and responded to it forcefully. Today, I look at the same message and realise that it did not merit a response at all, and I should have exercised restraint. But overall, despite the occasional slip, I have noticed an enhanced ability to exercise judgement, which I am happy about.

I now listen to—and watch—someone excited by the prospect of eating something special soon, perhaps ice cream. I see the anticipation and the increasing desire. That desire will be fulfilled. But not sated completely.

There is sorrow that a thrilling vacation, or an unusually

tasty meal, is over. The desire for another experience will germinate within, I know. This knowledge is itself a good thing and will temper my responses and expectations in a more sattvic way.

Now I am sensitive to what I eat, for example. The pickle I love, something else I do not enjoy—neither of these articulated responses truly have merit. I tell myself that food merely nourishes the body as I aspire for a higher goal. I need to exercise domination over my taste buds and pay minimal attention to the demands of my stomach.

Despite knowing this, I feel the need to enjoy the taste and comment on the food—salty, sweet, pungent and so on. They feed the gunas and create more karmic impulses. Sigh!

Now the memory of something bad I had done decades ago suddenly pulsates uncomfortably within. It was part of a "movie" that I had engaged with, which created a particular karmic seed. How do I successfully negate it in this lifetime? Or will I need to pay it forward in the next lifetime?

These kinds of thoughts now swirl within. I would say I am now quite sensitive to the entire drama of life. Thus, the seer, the real me, is slowly sensing the illusory nature of the seen through gradually enhanced discriminative intelligence (viveka). I certainly have a long way to go.

The firm hand of Patanjali guides me through his Yoga Sutras, helping me discern the ephemeral nature of everything while still showing me the direction. The journey will not be easy.

I will need to continuously mellow down my mind through attempts at austerity, self-study and an acceptance of a greater power that bears no wordy analysis. From there, Patanjali will show me the seven additional steps I need to understand and take.

Yes, I am the seer who reluctantly engages with the seen. If I am sincere, the seen will vanish soon.

The ego must go.

4

Engineering the Mind and Body

The Sadhana Pada declares that the principles of karma yoga are a powerful means of attaining samadhi. The mind is mellowed and replaced by humility and a deep sense of self-abnegation. Your mind swirls with the questions: Why do I need so much? Who exactly am I? Let me surrender to the most powerful and perfect entity, Ishwara.

It may also be inferred that it is a precursor to individual—but linked—disciplines that need to be mastered, which are now the focus of the remaining Sadhana Pada.

By practising each step, ignorance is overcome and spiritual advancement occurs. The kleshas are weakened and erased, and the seer no longer identifies with the seen. The quest requires single-minded focus and mastery over the distractions that continually attack the mind.

Sutras 29–43

Patanjali now lays out, in black and white, the seven steps to be mastered and continuously polished to attain the final, eighth step, samadhi. The need for each is vivid; they may be approached in sequence or as a continuous mix of practices. They cannot be skipped for any reason because of the tight interlocks between all of them.

- One: *Yama*, which deals with external observances
- Two: *Niyama*, one's own set of internal observances
- Three: *Asanas,* which deal with the need to keep one's body in perfect equilibrium and health
- Four: *Pranayama*, the management of breath, considered to contain the very essence of life
- Five: *Pratyahara*, mastery over the senses
- Six: *Dharana,* single-pointed focus on an appropriate object for the purpose of meditation
- Seven: *Dhyana,* meditation
- Eight: *Samadhi,* absorption

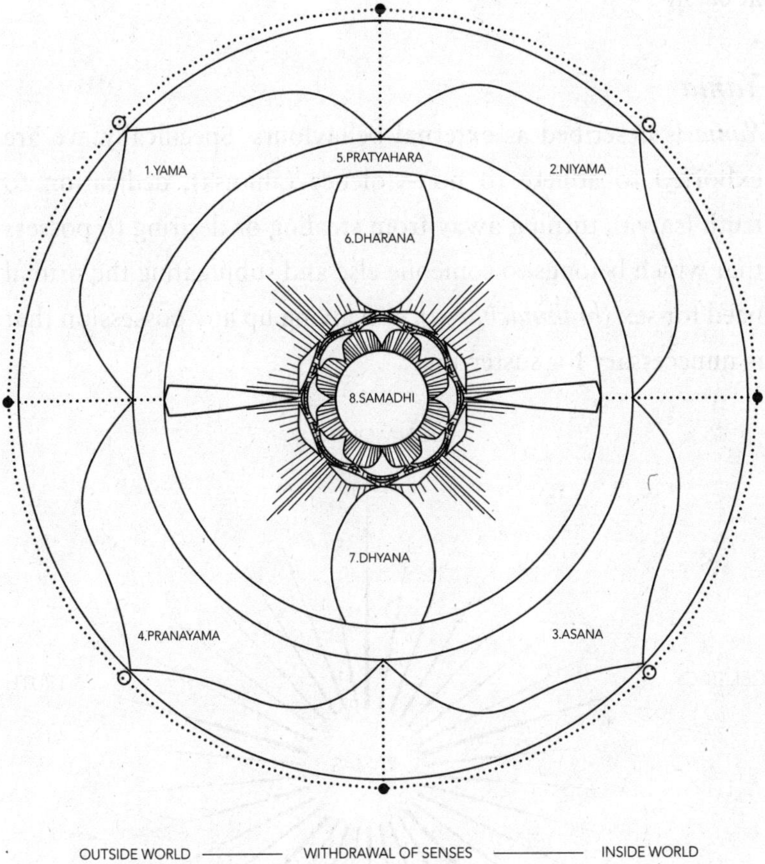

OUTSIDE WORLD —— WITHDRAWAL OF SENSES —— INSIDE WORLD

OUTSIDE WORLD	WITHDRAWAL OF SENSES	INSIDE WORLD
1.YAMA	5. PRATYAHARA	6.DHARANA
2.NIYAMA		7.DHYANA
3.ASANA		8.SAMADHI
4.PRANAYAMA		

Once the seven building blocks are understood and mastered, samadhi becomes possible. These interconnected "limbs" have their own deep contribution to make. Let's take a detailed look at each.

Yama

Yama is described as external behaviours. Specifically, we are exhorted to adhere to non-violence (ahimsa), dedication to truth (satya), turning away from stealing or desiring to possess that which belongs to someone else and subjugating the primal need for sex (*brahmacharya*), and giving up any possession that is unnecessary for sustenance.

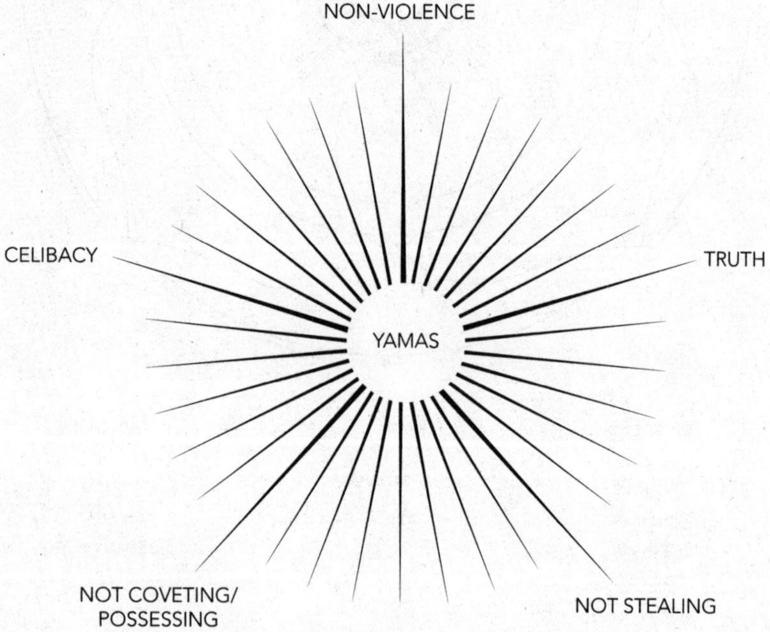

These principles are seen in various cultures around the world at diverse levels and so are not unique to India per se. But the point here, as far as yoga is concerned, is that stern observance of these behaviours leads to better self-management and a more sattvic interface with the world.

Ahimsa is India's great cultural and spiritual heritage, recognising the equality of all life and giving it equal respect. All beings love life itself, and it is necessary for us to respect this sentiment. Of course, violence can be in speech and thought, too, not just in action. The overriding point being that abjuring violence and the products of violence is a necessary step.

The Jains of India have taken it to great extents, wearing masks to prevent accidental entry of insects and walking barefoot to avoid trampling on living beings by mistake. The *Akaranga* sutras of the Jains speak numerous times about this matter. Here is one poetic extract:

> He who injures animals does not comprehend and renounce the sinful acts; he who does not injure these comprehends and renounces the sinful acts. Knowing them, a wise man should not act sinfully towards animals, nor cause others to act so, nor allow others to act so. He who knows these causes of sin relating to animals is called a reward-knowing sage.

Why would this be so? Perhaps an underlying belief that all life is one, that all consciousness is interconnected. Harming a living being that seeks to live is the same as damaging the collective consciousness. It is the same as hurting I, me, myself!

Someone practising yoga must therefore consider all his actions that might cause harm. It follows that eating meat becomes problematic. Notice that violence against animals translates to a tamasic matter.

This is a noble thought and exceedingly difficult to practise. But for a serious yogi, it is an essential and non-negotiable inclusion.

All who wish to be yogis must observe ahimsa in every dimension.

Satya translates to "truth"—in both words and thoughts. In other words, a perfect alignment between the two is expected. If there is misalignment, it can be expected that the kleshas are stimulated, adding further challenges and halting one's progress. Of course, there are many philosophical conundrums as to whether always speaking the truth is a good idea, especially when someone else's life is endangered when the truth is presented. However, the overriding principle is that the truth must be tempered with good judgement and kindness.

We may additionally deduce that ahimsa predominates as a necessary quality because one may technically speak the truth to mislead and harm someone.

Here is a simple example:

Your boss asks you: "Did you send that important email to Arun?"

He meant Arun Sharma.

You answer yes because you did indeed send it to Arun. So, it is the literal truth. But what *you* really meant was Arun Rao. At the same time, you are fully aware that your boss meant Arun Sharma. Your response was *not* an honest mistake. Therefore, you effectively lied as your intent was not right; you wanted to cover up that you did not do something you should have.

There is a story in the Mahabharata about precisely such a situation regarding the killing of Ashwathama. That was the name of a prince and was also the name of an elephant used as a vehicle in war. The death of Ashwathama was reported, but it was deliberately kept hidden that the reference was to the elephant and not the prince, who was the son of the great, invincible Drona. The intent was to mislead, and it worked. Drona was overcome with grief, thinking his son was killed. Thus, weakened and distracted, he too was killed.

Further, one must be careful in bluntly speaking the truth if it hurts another person's feelings. This example also places ahimsa on a higher pedestal. It does not excuse the uttering of falsehood but suggests judgement in its application.

The third yama enjoins you not to steal and not to even harbour the desire to possess something that belongs to someone else. If you do want something that belongs to someone else, you are presented with two options:

- One: curbing that desire, or
- Two, acting on it

If you act on it, you again commit an act of violence in thought and deed. Even if you do not act on it, distortion is introduced. You may still act on it in the future.

The best way to do this is to train your mind to not covet anything else to begin with. Therefore, this—and the last yama—is quite in sync with the first principles of kriya yoga that request minimalism.

The next yama, of celibacy, is particularly challenging. It is not only a matter of refraining from sexual activity but also controlling the base instinct that may invade the mind, quite similar in concept to avoiding stealing. The difference is that here, sensual desires are stimulated, whether through the act or by thinking of it, and cause disturbances to one's equanimity. This is a battle constantly fought and often lost because of the primal need that exists in all living beings to procreate. Being able to subdue it demonstrates the discipline needed on the path.

And finally, Patanjali again stresses minimalism: a directive that one should discard all possessions that serve no practical purpose. Acquiring them was probably a mistake in the first place because you yielded to your ego's desires to possess something, perhaps to make a point to yourself or to others, again falling into the trap of illusion.

But having recognised the futility of having more than you truly need, would you be willing to dispose of it?

Irrespective of your philosophical perspectives and conundrums, what-ifs, how-can-I's and buts, at the end of the day, Patanjali is clear: these are absolute vows you must take on yourself if samadhi is your destination.

There are no circumstances, no unusual times, no familial pressures, no geographical constraint and no occupational necessity that permits an exemption from the yamas for him who professes to be a yogi.

Try as one might, an ordinary person like me is likely to have transgressed every one of the yamas over a lifetime. Of course, one can argue that the pressures of life push us towards violating one or the other yama. But going forward, if you want to be a true yogi, you need to promise that you will observe these vows.

In the currents of life, one may be forced to indulge in certain acts—for example, a soldier cannot be non-violent. However, if a person claims to be a yogi, he cannot exercise any other option or claim an exception.

Ahimsa is the overriding principle.

Those then are the inviolable external observances required of a yogi.

Niyama

Patanjali now begins the journey inwards. He refers to the following as matters of personal internal discipline:

- One: **Cleanliness** of one's external body and of what is ingested
- Two: **Satisfaction or contentment with one's state,** suggesting that hankering for anything more is automatically an acceptance of the need for pleasure
- Three: **Austerity** or **minimalism** (this comes up often), suggesting that one's material needs must be minimised
- Four: **Self-study** and the study of scriptures to gain inspiration
- Five: **Surrender to Ishwara** in the belief that the Supreme Power knows best

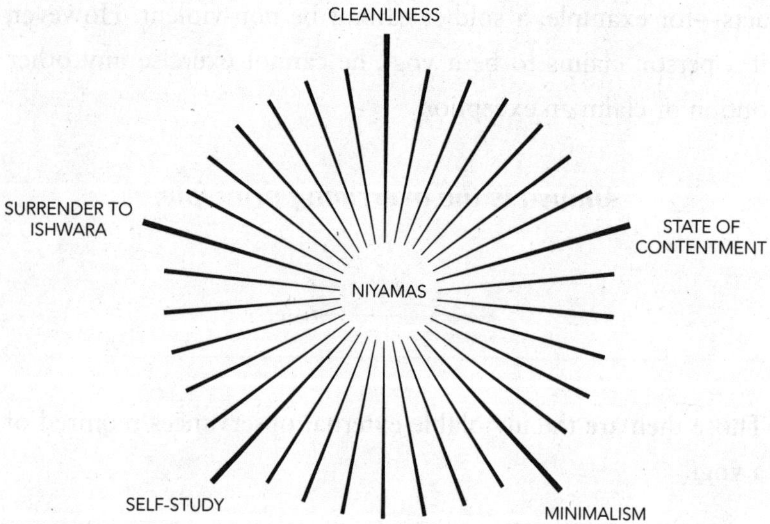

You may see here an inward movement as the journey progresses. The yamas are external observances, and the niyamas are more focused on internal qualities to aspire for.

Of cleanliness, one seeks the ideal, of course, but milestones include the body and the mind, both of which may serve as distractions.

What does it mean to be satisfied and content? Clearly, a term like external ambition has no place in a yogi's dictionary. Neither is sloth. Here we say that a person is at peace with their current state of existence and aspires for nothing that does not come on its own.

How difficult that is in practice, with peer pressure and other external stimulus commanding you to demand more and ask for more and directly suggesting that dissatisfaction is an excellent quality! But if you are satisfied with whatever you have, possessing little and wanting nothing has its own pure beauty.

Satisfaction is easily attained by possessing little and wanting little.

The recurring theme of self-study, seeking peace and solitude, and reading and understanding oneself is striking. These then lead to the other theme, surrendering to Ishwara and developing a sense of humility, seeking nothing for oneself.

Now that we have a reference, it becomes easier to have a mental alarm system. If contrary thoughts and principles rear up or beckon, we now know there is a better, cleaner and simpler alternative!

Contrary thoughts that seek to invade our thinking include violence. Patanjali is clear that the "supply chain" of violence stretches beyond the one who commits violence to the one who connives in it and gets some benefit, to any degree. A calm person does not commit violence. A violent person is triggered by greed, anger or delusion of various intensities.

And extending this point further, once one masters non-violence in thought and deed, there is no possibility of nurturing enmity. It becomes an unacceptable option.

But what is beautiful is that a non-violent individual's equanimity rubs off on others too. This is a very profound thought, suggesting that a person's temperament affects the temperament of everyone around! If your workplace or home seems tense, who is the real source? If the environment is peaceful and calm, where is this coming from?

It is a fact that animals are calm in the presence of one who is imbued with the light of non-violence. When people claim a particular dog is "aggressive", it is certain that the human owner is aggressive too.

In a separate book, I have written, quite coincidentally, about a mother whispering into the ears of her newborn child:

I must sow the seeds of humility in your heart early on, that you use the material world merely for sustenance, never forgetting that you can take nothing away when your time comes.

"Death. Can it really come?" I wonder, uncomprehending even as I say those words. What savage twist of destiny and inevitable fate can already claim you for death when your vibrant little life refreshes me and those who look upon you lovingly?

These jewels that you see on me are not what they seem. They represent knowledge, justice, compassion and devotion.

And Patanjali continues in this vein, stating firmly that as a yogi, the qualities possessed rub off everywhere. And it also generates unusual powers. For example, a yogi committed to speaking the truth may say something (not arbitrary) that others are impelled to make true. Thus, if an unselfish yogi looks into your eyes and says, "Be good", you are likely to be affected by his words and act accordingly.

And a yogi who has no interest in stealing automatically attracts the trust of others. In the simplest case, he attracts wealth, in which he is not interested. In other instances, he attracts the good wishes and invaluable respect of others, which count for more than material wealth.

Lastly, the yogi committed to celibacy generates great power to manifest, a power that will be touched upon in a subsequent chapter.

In the same vein, extending the principle, the yogi who has absolutely no interest in possessions of any kind gains great insights into the dimensions of past and future births, says Patanjali. This is because he seeks to gain nothing from such knowledge.

Whatever you give up as a yogi,
you gain in other myriad ways.

Having discovered that the physical body is fundamentally flawed, unsatisfactory and prone to degeneration, a yogi realises that being attached to it has no meaning. Beneath the soap-scrubbed external facade of your body lie noxious bubbling fluids, excreta, and a restless set of delicately connected biological mechanisms that will ultimately fail. This has dawned on the yogi, and he proceeds accordingly.

Likewise, he sees that others exist in unsatisfactory physical sheaths and does not see any merit in contact of any kind. This, too, is an advanced state of dispassion and disinterest. The body has no intrinsic merit, we conclude, but must be endured or used as a vehicle to gain samadhi and kept clean.

The process of cleanliness also applies to the mind. Sattvic thoughts—balanced, mild, light and positive—will prevail. The mind is alert, positive, focused, fit and flexible, capable of controlling the senses and now ready to continue the passage inward. There is no desire for material objects or sensual gratification. There is a clear understanding of the body's impermanence, and the yogi is content that there is nothing to be gained elsewhere, externally. From this understanding and satisfaction, the true state of happiness is reached.

Thus, moving from minimalism and simple living, keeping your body clean and healthy, and ensuring your mind is clean, too, filled with sattvic thoughts, the body and mind move upwards to their maximum potential.

What a great description of the rigorous disciplines! This understanding—and the sincere application—of the yamas and niyamas creates the perfect canvas for subsequent practices.

This is what I absorbed from sutras 29 through 43 of the Sadhana Pada:

- There are seven steps to master while moving towards the eighth, samadhi.
- Non-negotiable disciplines like truth, non-stealing, disinterest in possessions and celibacy give great powers. Ahimsa, in thought and deed, is the overriding discipline to be followed.
- When cleanliness in body and mind are scrupulously followed, they are made perfect.

Sutras 44–55

The yamas and niyamas provide the first tangible milestones for the aspirant to achieve. Tough as they are, and almost impossible to completely master, they are nonetheless something that needs to be kept vividly alive on one's awareness radar as one begins the journey towards the eventual goal of samadhi.

With strict outward practice and internal observances, with ahimsa in thought, speech and action constantly underlined, Patanjali takes us forward, points out the obvious unsatisfactory nature of the body and the mind, and recommends keeping it clean. By doing so, we inch closer to noble and exalted thoughts, towards an ideal state of comprehension of the mind and body.

We shed so many things along the way in terms of attitudes, opinions and desires; the ego finds itself abandoned in many ways.

The mind now leans toward understanding more, and here Patanjali tells us to study the sacred texts for additional light and inspiration. By focusing on one's deity, where the mind tends to be most reverential, the mind is tuned and shuns distractions.

In our traditions, a specific deity often has a particular attraction. It appears as a source of strength and has a specific meaning for an individual. We call this deity the *ishta-devata*. Patanjali recognises the human need to feel distinct in some way and turns it around to recommend connecting to this "personal deity" via a diligent study of the scriptures. This is, in my opinion, a clever way to gain the cooperation of the aspirant by leveraging the unconscious weight and shadow of traditions.

Using this method, the aspirant attains samadhi as a kind of acceleration. Patanjali mentions several times that surrendering to Ishwara in every way is necessary for the end goal. However, this is not necessarily an alternate path; we can interpret it to mean that surrendering to Ishwara while perfecting all the other limbs (yama, niyama, asana, pranayama, pratyahara, dharana and dhyana) is necessary to attain samadhi. In particular, the feeling of devotion must act as a supporting blanket over all the other practices.

Devotion to one's object of spiritual succour is the motif across all the limbs of yoga.

Asana

Much has been written (and misunderstood) about asanas, the set of physical postures that are immensely popular. There are 84 defined ones seen in two major texts, the *Goraksha Sataka* and the 15th century *Hatha Yoga Pradipika,* and many practitioners (like me) innovate in their practice and enjoy mixing them up and creating our own hybrid asanas. Asana practice is recommended to keep fit and be optimally healthy. All this is true.

Patanjali, in this section of his discourse, finally speaks

of asanas—the third and most well-known discipline—in a very cryptic way. He says that "the asana should be still and pleasant".

Is this contrary to popular practice? Perhaps. But it may be useful to step back and understand why asana practice is recommended at all.

Recall that external and internal observances (yama and niyama) were the first two stages of establishing a mental rigour of sorts. Keeping in view the later practices emphasising long stretches of meditation, the perfection of asanas is logical for this reason: the need to hold steady for a prolonged period.

If the body is not fit, meditation will falter. The aspirant will be in a state of continuous discomfort, constantly adjusting his seated posture. The body has not been trained to enjoy extended periods of quiet and focused breathing (pranayama, to be discussed later) while being in a state of balance and focus.

Asanas indeed serve to train the body for calm focus. A simple principle is that if the mind is agitated, bodily balance is unachievable. Those who are otherwise used to asanas as part of their regimen will understand the point immediately. Try to stand motionless, and you will discover it is exceedingly difficult. The body totters, shakes, shivers and sways. Close your eyes and try it again and see how you almost fall.

Asana practice underlines slow and steady melding of the mind and body through steady and calm breathing. Any asana practice that causes the aspirant to inhale and exhale quickly and laboriously as though experiencing discomfort or tension is flawed.

Asanas train the body and mind to be still, impervious to distractions.

Many aspirants also close their eyes during their practice to further block out sensory distractions; I do this often. No matter how complex and strange an asana looks, it has not been mastered unless the practitioner is seen to be calm and her breathing is slow and steady.

This obviously requires extended practice and dedication. Yoga—as conventionally understood—is not a physical fitness technique but has a different goal. It may happen that extended practice results in a lithe and healthy body, but that is, in fact, incidental. The practitioner wishes to meditate for extended periods, still and calm. Without a strong physical frame that supports focus and does not find any posture uncomfortable in the least, one-point meditation is impossible. Distractions caused by the body seeking comfort will plague the mind. Each cell seems to call out for attention—scratch me here, shift me there, straighten me out and so on.

Asanas do require singular focus on various parts of the body and close attention to the state of individual muscles. Some are relaxed, some stiff, some are effectively atrophied due to disuse. One who keeps himself fit and supple through dedicated asana practice is ready for more arduous and demanding meditation sessions.

A yogi whose face radiates tranquillity while in the most demanding posture has understood the point. His breathing is slow and steady, his brow is smooth. His eyes are likely to be closed, but they are peaceful and calm if open. He has additionally surrendered to Ishwara, and therefore, asana practice may be considered a form of worship. There is no pain and no discomfort, and after some time, the mind is no longer even aware of the body.

You may have observed that when your body is in discomfort, it tends to have shallow breaths. Thus, a body in the ideal asana posture ought to be at peace and be relatively indifferent to externalities like heat and cold. Breathing is slow, deep and smooth.

My asana teacher used to ask me to "observe the pain and discomfort". Far from being dramatic, observing pain reduces it or makes it bearable. The act of neutrally observing one's pain is a stark example of the separation of the seer and the seen, referred to earlier.

The presence of pain is indicative of other problems that need to be investigated. As breathing becomes slow and steady, pain either effectively disappears or becomes bearable. It is not easy, as everyone's pain threshold is different. Nevertheless, in most cases, if the focus shifts, with determination, from wincing with pain to breathing slowly and regularly, pain becomes tolerable, even if uncomfortable.

Once again, we see how the mind can be trained to be focused, a critical prerequisite to long-drawn meditative inquiry.

Every asana must be an experience of deep peace and slow and even breathing.

This extract from one of my stories illustrates the idea:

> See the Yogi in Vrikshasana, balancing perfectly on one leg in the waters of the sacred river at dawn, while raising his arms above him, his palms together and his eyes closed in contemplation.
>
> The icy water tests his resolve; his will is too strong. His body is still and does not sway in the cold wind. His mind does not experience currents and eddies; the flowing waters have absorbed them from him.
>
> The Yogi prepares for the journey towards samadhi.

Pranayama

It is easy to see how effective practices of the first three limbs—yama, niyama and asanas—create the ideal crucible for the next critical preparatory skill—pranayama.

An ancient theory holds that *prana* is the life-force, entering our body through the breath. Pranayama translates to the regulation of prana.

As mentioned earlier, shallow and rapid breathing is a clear giveaway of an agitated or troubled mind. Patanjali has pointed to the incredible value to be gained by regulating inhalation, exhalation and halting the process of breathing.

Some say that pranayama has more than 120 variants.

However, in general, the idea is to observe the slow inhalation of air through the nostril, cease the movement and then exhale slowly, only to cease again. This can only be done by tuning your mind to the process, showing the ability of pranayama to help you focus. The moment you lose focus because your mind wanders, the smoothness of breathing is affected.

Why then does the affected mind cause breathing to be disturbed? Here we refer again to the gunas called tamas and rajas that cause thoughts to distract the mind. In the instant inhalation or exhalation sees a change, meditation is affected.

Breath holds the secret.

This practice requires immense dedication through which patience is fostered and equanimity is reached. Changing the period of inhalation, exhalation and holding of the movement is a desirable feature.

Here is a table to help you begin the practice:

Slow Inhale	Hold	Slow Exhale	Hold	Slow Inhale	Hold	Slow Exhale	Hold
1 sec.	4 sec.	2 sec.	4 sec.	1 sec.	4 sec.	2 sec.	4 sec.

Pranayama induces calm. Consequently, we see that the heart beats at a slower rate during this practice. There can be no doubt that the connection between breathing, the mind and the body is extremely tight. Over time, it may be possible to do two or three cycles of this *inhale-cease-exhale-cease* breathing continuum in a minute, as opposed to about 12 to 16 for normal involuntary breathing that most of us are completely unaware of.

But what if you could suspend breathing for much longer periods? What if you could do an inhalation–exhalation cycle once every ten minutes or ten hours? Or several days?

Impossible, did you say? Hold on!

A fourth type of pranayama that only very advanced practitioners can do is to cease inhalation and exhalation completely. The body is nourished by prana alone, which moves in and out of the nostrils. There are numerous historical references to yogis suspending breathing completely for days on end and emerging from their experience without a problem.

Claude Wade speaks of his experience in witnessing the reviving of an ascetic, Haridas, in the company of Maharajah Ranjeet Singh in Lahore, in 1837. Haridas had apparently suspended breathing for forty days and had been watched over carefully by guards. This is an extract from an account where Claude Wade describes what he saw:

> The legs and arms of the body were shrivelled and stiff, the face full, the head reclining on the shoulder like that of a corpse. I then called to the medical gentleman who was attending me to come down and inspect the body, which he did, but could discover no pulsation in the heart, the temples, or the arm. There was, however, a heat about the region of the brain, which no other part of the body exhibited.

There are other accounts of such advanced practitioners of yoga who find even the natural need to breathe unnecessary. In the *Vishnu Purana*, Dhruva is said to have mastered yogic breathing and stopped breathing while focusing on God to gain his blessings, which he did.

But in summary, mastering breathing and transforming the activity from an involuntary to a voluntary one is immensely demanding and must be preceded by the other disciplines. By thus mastering breathing, Patanjali avers that the overall skein of ignorance is significantly weakened, and true knowledge, which goes beyond words and teaching, is ready to shine forth.

All these (arduous) practices, with specific emphasis on pranayama, create conditions perfect for concentration. There are no distractions, mental or physical, to be concerned about at this stage. Yama, niyama and asanas have also contributed to the perfect practice of pranayama.

And now, at this stage, the fifth limb, pratyahara, is accessed.

Pratyahara

Such tremendous discipline, starting from the kriya yoga principles through the first four limbs, has prepared the mind to this point. The objects that sense the external world (the eyes, skin, ears, nose and tongue) and affect the mind are no longer required. They ought to be withdrawn from service, as it were.

Notice that the sense objects provoke immediate responses

from us as they attempt to create an imbalance in our gunas, lowering sattva and raising the proportion of rajas and tamas.

The nose smells. The tongue tastes. The skin feels. The eyes see. The ears hear. As they continue their "duty", they add to our sense of identity.

Can you smell jasmine and be unaffected? If you are affected, why? Was it a pleasant childhood memory?

Can the aromas from the kitchen leave you indifferent? Why does your mouth water in anticipation? Did it remind you of something your mother used to make?

Do the thorns on a rose stem bother you as they brush against your arm? Why?

Can you stop from turning in the direction of a loud sound? Why not? Was the sound harsh?

Can you be indifferent to the scenic beauty of the Himalayas as the setting sun paints them with shades of red and orange? Why not?

In all these cases, what can you do to break the association with the sense organs?

The senses must be trained to not react when stimulated.

This ability to decline to react to sensory impulses is only feasible after the mastery of pranayama. This is called pratyahara and is the next stage in evolution for the disciplined yogi.

The mind is bombarded by sensory impulses that crave attention. But self-discipline has now reached such a level that it is possible to train oneself to further ignore the images that they—the senses—present to your mind.

This is the entry portal for the journey within. Though it is usually placed in the *bahiranga* set (to be described later), it could equally be placed as a stand-alone limb because it serves as a bridge between the outside and the inside. (This matter will be alluded to towards the end of the next section on the Vibhuti Pada.)

At this stage, Patanjali is satisfied. As all external factors are subdued and effectively ignored, the mind can now concentrate without distractions. The problem of samskaras or latent impressions does persist, but a person of determination can overcome them with effort.

The Sadhana Pada closes at this stage, covering the first five limbs, priming us for the subsequent three.

What an astonishingly perceptive and structured analysis of everything we need to do if we wish to truly meditate and withdraw within!

One by one, human frailties of the mind and body are identified, subdued and conquered, or at least managed firmly. The outside must be blocked, the inside must be spotless and the supporting body ready and able to help you. The breath must be understood and mastered, and the senses must no longer sense.

All sensory experiences are now cosmically irrelevant. Taste, discomfort, heat, anger—they are now seen as being distractions for the journey.

These then are my learnings from sutras 44 through 55 of the Sadhana Pada:

- Asanas prepare the body for deep and extended meditation; each asana must be held for an extended period while breathing slowly.
- Pranayama, or breath management, is the gateway to the inner world.
- Mastering the senses is the last step needed to move inwards and meditate.

What I learnt from Sutras 29 through 55 of the Sadhana Pada

The Sadhana Pada goes into extraordinary detail regarding the expectations from a yogi. Such superhuman discipline and self-control across all dimensions of the human condition! I certainly wondered if I had it in me.

External observances are challenging. That is an understatement—it involves great introspection and challenges practically every response we have been giving to the world thus far.

We live in a complex world of interconnected social links. We depend on others. Others depend on us. We have been brainwashed with the principles of aggressive survival and existence over the millennia; these are now our instinct. Braggadocio, and a need to keep ahead of everyone else, fertilises the principle of violence in thought, words and action.

Yet, to be a yogi and move towards samadhi, I am required to unlearn socially admired qualities and swim in a countercurrent.

Ahimsa had always appealed to me as a concept. But again, the primal need to survive in and dominate a hostile environment had made me, like any other, believe that the principle of "survival of the fittest" is a practical matter.

Now, I need to rethink my animus towards some I had poor prior experiences with, even if those thoughts were always within my head and never expressed. I admit I "hated" a few people for certain acts; this was a grave failing. Going forward, am I capable of relinquishing such thoughts and truly practice ahimsa? Time will tell.

As I extended the radius and area of my thoughts, I saw that violence has been an underlying theme, even if not obvious. The consumption of animal products involves a secondary or tertiary act of violence; not being aware of the links can no longer be an excuse. My demand for wool or milk involves condoning an act against a sentient being that wishes to live unharmed. The terror and fear that my demand creates, even if I am far away from the specific act of violence, is unacceptable.

To what extent could my observance of ahimsa go?

The beauty of the principles of ahimsa is deeply embedded in the ethos of India. As I've mentioned earlier, the Jains have closely examined this sophisticated thought to its greatest granularity. But in general, considering the motive and the consequences to oneself is of paramount value, with the act being secondary.

Who can claim to have always been truthful in all matters? A little half-truth here, silence somewhere else, some exaggeration elsewhere—these are the expected behaviours that a "normal" person deploys to thrive, survive and succeed.

Have I stolen in my life? Yes, I have. I cannot defend myself by saying everyone has done so, whether they admit it or not.

I remember one such deliberate act committed in school when I was a young child testing the limits of what I could get away with. It is astonishing that I have not forgotten and continue to feel ashamed decades after the event. My classmate never knew, and he has vanished into the mists of time. I can only ask for his forgiveness in my mind and hope that the prayer carries to him somehow, wherever he is.

Of course, this is just one instance. I cannot write down the long list of unfortunate acts that I have wilfully committed. I will take that one example as something to illustrate the long reach of the uncomfortable memory of an incorrect act.

Minimalism is relatively easy, so I would like to believe. Do I live a simple life because I must or because I want to? I think the latter, at this stage of my life. The fewer the possessions, the greater the contentment. What can you steal from someone who has nothing? What pleasure will I get from clinging on to things that will continue to exist after I am gone?

Yes, I believe I have reached that stage of minimalism with a few aberrations. I hope I continue along that path, looking at all potential possessions with the keen knowledge that their true value to my inner self is zero.

Once you consider austerity and minimalism as a desirable matter, actual material needs become restricted to only basics. There is no need whatsoever to take on whatever is luxury and pointless fluff. Patanjali's observation is that those who relinquish or do not covet end up attracting "greater riches". That can be understood to mean peace of mind, greater balance and an understanding that sorrow can be erased by removing the veil of ignorance that wraps us.

As a very simple illustration: I do not charge when I teach

music. It may appear to be a dramatic gesture, but it has profoundly impacted my own ability to understand music at a deeper level. This is the "payback" I have received, perhaps.

Attraction to others also reduces to impulses traceable to an imbalance in the three gunas. It is to be viewed from the point of the ego. The seer deep within looks at the other through a distorted lens and imagines an identification with the seen. But nothing is further from the truth. It may well go against base instincts but that is the point: the mind must prevail and recognise attraction for what it is; transient and ultimately a source of sorrow since the mind craves repeated experiences that may not be possible.

Cleanliness as a concept is so profound. On the one hand, it is obvious because our senses detect the unclean. But it goes beyond and into the private recesses of our selves.

I have observed that I am now slightly more organised in my personal matters. I even clean the area in which I do my asana practice every morning, as I am aware of how everything is now linked. Trivial examples, one might say, but the idea of keeping things clean has its own cascading power. Layers of dust cover our minds too. As I remove them, a little at a time, I see a spark of my true self deep within, uncluttered by worldly experiences. And from this exercise germinates the desire to be alone and find happiness in it.

This is not always possible because others depend on me in several ways, but I can say that there is greater contentment in solitude. Therefore, I look upon my interaction with the world as fulfilling duties to others without the expectation of appreciation or rewards.

Contentment—yes, I am content in solitude, in my state of existence as an ordinary man who lives a regular life, and in asanas.

I spend at least an hour every morning doing asanas. I am moderately adept.

Now, after absorbing Patanjali's wisdom, my practice involves greater awareness. This awareness extends to individual muscle strands and various parts of my body to a very granular level. As a result, the mind is calmer and attaining the postures, no matter how difficult, is done with greater awareness, gentle inhalation and exhalation, and focus.

I have truly understood that the mind can prevail over matter. The mind very slowly scans every square inch of my body. In cases where I need to bend, for instance, I move my awareness to the area about my tailbone and cajole my muscles into yielding as I exhale. Over time, the stressed muscle yields and I can complete the asana. And in that posture, I find great contentment in following the slow movement of my breath as it enters and exits my nostrils.

Even *shirshasana*, the headstand, which I do with reasonable competence, is now packaged with two components:

- Closed eyes to block out visual stimulation that might upset my balance
- Very slow inhalation and exhalation

In the initial days of asana practice, I was driven, with excitement and false pride, by the intent of conquering the posture. As a result, my breath faltered and was irregular. I did not understand then that smooth breathing was also critically important.

But now, I realise that weight must be given in equal measure to both. When that happens, the body is still, perfectly balanced and content. As Patanjali says in sutra 46: the body must be comfortable and relaxed (in the most complex of postures).

This is the new ideal.

Patanjali's stress on pranayama in the latter parts of the Sadhana Pada awoke a dormant interest I had in the matter.

As I decelerate in all matters due to age and experience, my attention has also shifted to my breath. An odd thing to happen, one might say, especially since I have been practising asanas for decades now. But all things take their own time to ripen and emerge.

The time after asanas is spent controlling the intake and exit of breath. I observe many things now: the passage of time for the movement, the temperature, the texture and the volume.

Obviously, the mind becomes focused on this act.

The air moves in as I inhale. Then I stop, "watching" the fresh air being absorbed and the body give up "old" air. Then I exhale. The air is warm but equally smooth. Then I stop, giving my lungs some rest.

Who could have imagined that the act of breathing could be so interesting and absorbing? Who could have imagined that inhalation and exhalation could involve so many parts of the body?

Now it is clear that extra-long inhalations and exhalations, and the protracted holding of the breath, is vivid, introspective and ultimately beneficial to my quest. There is the gentle rushing of air moving in and out. Longer, very relaxed retentions. What joy!

And obviously, it helps in putting all the prior limbs of yoga that Patanjali has spoken about in a better perspective. Each is independent, and all are interlinked too. Pranayama adds a new layer of awareness while I do asanas, and the mind dwells thoughtfully on the yamas and niyamas. Each stands alone while strengthening the others.

I inhale better thoughts and exhale negativity.

Pratyahara, while initially appearing unreasonably idealistic, no longer seems unsurmountable.

I realise that the five senses are roadblocks. I do not need to indulge them. I do not react spontaneously with utter pleasure or disgust when the senses present something to me.

Observances, physical alertness, mental strength, breath control, self-management—the list of terms I need to fully assimilate is growing.

I am no longer in awe of them. However, I understand the challenges they pose for someone who walks the streets of Bangalore alone, like so many others in different cities, surrounded by dust, din, garbage, advertisements, anger and sorrow.

I shall find myself within.

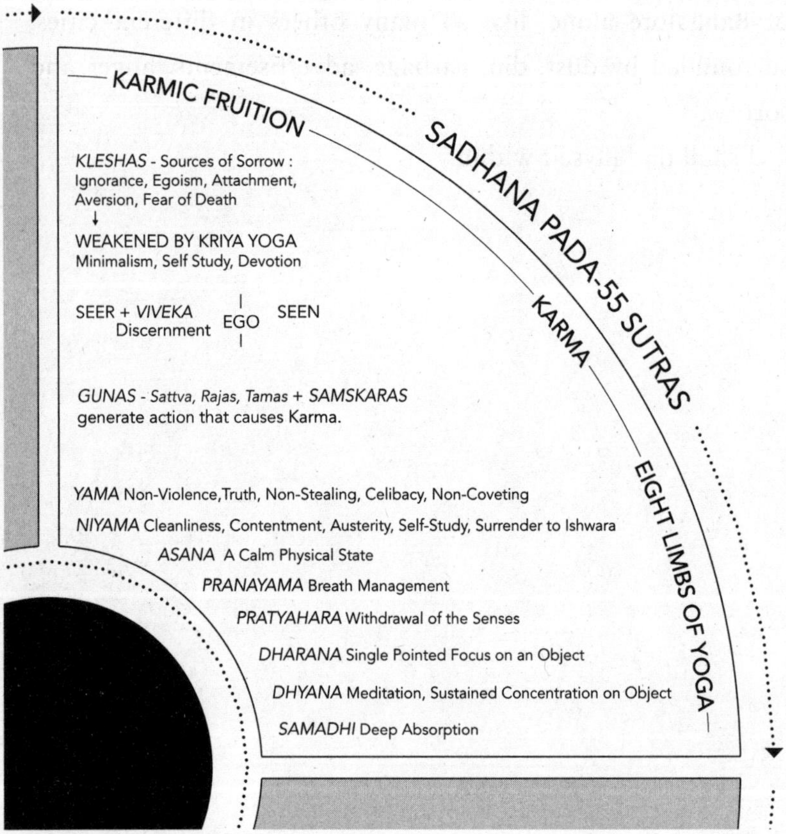
KARMIC FRUITION
SADHANA PADA-55 SUTRAS
KLESHAS - Sources of Sorrow :
Ignorance, Egoism, Attachment,
Aversion, Fear of Death
WEAKENED BY KRIYA YOGA
Minimalism, Self Study, Devotion
SEER + VIVEKA
Discernment
EGO
SEEN
KARMA
GUNAS - Sattva, Rajas, Tamas + SAMSKARAS
generate action that causes Karma.
EIGHT LIMBS OF YOGA
YAMA Non-Violence,Truth, Non-Stealing, Celibacy, Non-Coveting
NIYAMA Cleanliness, Contentment, Austerity, Self-Study, Surrender to Ishwara
ASANA A Calm Physical State
PRANAYAMA Breath Management
PRATYAHARA Withdrawal of the Senses
DHARANA Single Pointed Focus on an Object
DHYANA Meditation, Sustained Concentration on Object
SAMADHI Deep Absorption

Section 3

The Power—Vibhuti Pada

5

Exploring Mental Alchemy

We now step into the mystical Vibhuti Pada.

Here we shall learn how the diligent yogi acquires certain abilities that seem, at first, incredible. A friend once said he found it a bit scary. "Are we talking about magic and superstition?" he asked with a slightly nervous laugh.

If we lack the ability to understand and explain something, we might consider it dark and mysterious and perhaps become even a little apprehensive. You may encounter unusual themes and ideas as we progress through this section. Of course, there's much more to consider, as we shall see. But first, let's do a recap. How did we arrive here?

Patanjali's discourse has been intellectually exhilarating. The systematic and thorough treatment of yoga is breathtaking in its diligence and in the way the human mind is analysed.

We learn in the Samadhi Pada that the true intent of life is to merge into the Infinite Reality via samadhi. Two types of processes of attaining samadhi have been described. Potential distractions have been enumerated, and meditation has been prescribed as a means to still the mind that is in constant flux. "Om" has also been presented as an option to approach the Supreme, Ishwara. We understood what we needed to strive towards.

After that, the Sadhana Pada starts by describing the principles of kriya yoga and then moves on to list the challenges we will encounter, not the least being ignorance. The gunas are described as an unstable mix of qualities that present pictures to the delusional mind; the seer mistakenly identifies with what he sees and must struggle hard to sever the connection.

Patanjali continues the discourse of the Sadhana Pada by describing the eight limbs of yoga. Yamas and niyamas are intended to inculcate discipline in the way we interface with the world and seek perfection within. The asanas, which ought to be practised while breathing slowly and smoothly, are intended to prepare the body for prolonged meditation.

Thereafter, pranayama brings us to a deep understanding of the magic of breath, where focusing on it helps to develop greater self-awareness. Finally, by defusing the potency of the senses, so to say, via pratyahara, interaction with the external physical world is minimised to practically nothing.

There stops the engagement with the tangible reality. These five limbs of Patanjali's principles are collectively called *bahiranga*.

And now, we cross the bridge and move inwards!

In the enchanting Vibhuti Pada, Patanjali continues with the last three limbs of yoga that move inwards: dharana, dhyana and the final state of samadhi, which has been previously described in considerably greater detail in the section by the same name.

These three limbs are collectively called antaranga. This graphic explains the concepts from left to right:

Yama	**Niyama**	**Asana**	**Pranayama**	**Pratyahara**	**Dharana**	**Dhyana**	**Samadhi**
External–Sadhana Pada					Internal–Vibhuti Pada		
Bahiranga					Antaranga		

As I mentioned right in the beginning, the Vibhuti Pada interestingly focuses on what is often called "supernatural" powers, though, as we shall see, the term is misleading. An extremely sophisticated understanding of the subtleties and potential of mind and matter are expounded on.

Sutras 1–15

In his brilliant style that speaks of precise structuring and a gradual unveiling, much as a perceptive and patient guru might reveal knowledge to a novice student, Patanjali now explains what the last three limbs mean.

Dharana

Dharana is described in simple terms as fixing the mind on one place or object. Of course, the object may be real—say a candle—or imaginary: a picture in your mind. This is a practice aid, preparatory to the next step. Can you focus on an object and slowly reduce external interference and inducements?

Prima facie, this is not very difficult, as most of us have learnt to concentrate on specific matters while engaged in other activities. Dancers, musicians and artists have all learnt to focus on the matter at hand to perform at their best. Do we not, for example, often concentrate well when writing an exam? We know what would happen if we did not!

When I was a young boy, I thoroughly enjoyed practising my violin for long hours. The results were good.

But when it came to certain subjects at school, my mind would wander, and I would stare out of the window and be lost in daydreaming. The results were not good!

I digress. We are not speaking of dharana in routine matters but in the context of the eight limbs of yoga.

The requirement here is to focus after mastering the first five limbs. Why? Because doing so would bring forward a clear and clean mind and body, no longer distracted by externalities. If you were to try without the preparation that Patanjali prescribes, you would see that such concentration is difficult to sustain for more than a few seconds, while the mind quickly yields to distractions outside and inside. In true dharana, the sustaining is longer, and great internal strength is applied to block out pinpricks to the mind.

The mind makes every effort to focus on the flickering, unsteady flame from a lamp. And it too flickers, just like the flame.

(As an aside, recall that these ideas have been alluded to in the last few sutras of the Samadhi Pada as samprajnata.)

Becoming adept at dharana is a slow process. If you are interested, you might wish to start trying it for short periods, gradually increasing the duration over a few weeks. The table below might be useful. Accept the fact that the mind will wander almost immediately. Catch it and bring it back firmly! Unless you try with sincerity, you will not know what you are capable of!

Week	Duration
1	30 seconds
2	45 seconds
3	60 seconds
4-8	2 minutes

Dhyana

Dharana holds the idea that "I am focusing on THAT object." But as this ability is enhanced, the distinction starts vanishing. The idea becomes: "I and the object are becoming one." Single-point focus is now enhanced to a kind of continuous flow. This is dhyana.

The mind's efforts are rewarded; even the flame seems steady as though controlled by the mind. The periods of uninterrupted focus become longer and longer.

Samadhi

Finally, in samadhi, the distinction is completely lost. Individual identity loses conceptual meaning for the yogi.

If you recall, the state of samadhi has been described in great detail in the first section, so there is no need to repeat it here.

So, let's summarise.

- Dharana > Let me concentrate on that object
- Dhyana> I am dissolving in that object
- Samadhi > There is no distinction between the object and I

The flame burns bright; the yogi's individual identity is subsumed. The goal of the yogi has been reached.

Patanjali now informs me that once this sequential process—samyama—is traversed, I, as a yogi, will gain true insight into many matters. The process and a few types of samadhi have been referenced earlier too. As I practise samyama, I am told that I will gain greater and greater insights into my true nature and a clearer indication of what lies ahead.

When dharana, dhyana and samadhi are progressively and sequentially practised, the action is called samyama.

Intriguing!

You may notice that there are various, gradually escalating types of samadhi mentioned in the Samadhi Pada. Patanjali states that this process of samyama must be repeated, again and again, to move to higher levels of samadhi.

A piercing observation follows that is spiritually incisive: the antaranga of one type of samadhi is the bahiranga of the next level of samadhi!

I would describe it as a mathematical amusement:

Bahiranga of Samadhi (X+1) = Antaranga of Samadhi (X)

Where X is a samadhi variant at one level and X+1 is the samadhi variant at the next level.

In other words, the inward-looking practices of a "lower"

samadhi are the external practices of a "higher" samadhi.

To illustrate, *sabija* samadhi is external to *nirbija* samadhi and nirbija samadhi is external to *dharma-megha* samadhi, which is described eloquently in the Kaivalya Pada at the very end.

This "equation" (it's not really an equation; it's just some mild humour for the reader who likes mathematics!) resolves itself when asamprajnata samadhi is achieved. In other words, there are no external assists; we seek nirbija samadhi, or that without a seed. (Though, as suggested in the previous paragraph, a glorious state of dharma-megha samadhi exists thereafter. Let us wait to read about it in the Kaivalya Pada.)

This process cannot be fast-tracked. It requires decades of awareness and practice. At the same time, this is not an abstract idea. All this is achievable to you, dear reader.

The antaranga of one type of samadhi is the bahiranga of a higher state of samadhi.

Let me share an extract from one of my stories, "Within My Depths", that may have relevance, even if in a creative way:

> I have now drifted one layer below the conscious level.
>
> About me is a peculiar murmur and weightlessness.
>
> A haze of light seems visible just above the clearly

distinguishable separating layer between where I was and where I am. I twist and turn very slowly and without effort. I peer down at the darkness of the layers that beckon below, inviting me to dive in. I can hear an urgent shouting. I control the breathing of the body to which I belong, though I have somehow separated from it while still being trapped within it.

I now slowly move down one more level. I am reminded of a hot-air balloon descending through layers of air. As I now enter this new layer, there is great calm and quiet around. The ink-black surroundings seem very safe. I can see very well indeed, and there is a profound sense of peace. I did not know that within me, there had been such depths and layers that invited exploration. I am still conscious of my heart beating gently in the distance.

I close my eyes and then close them again and again. Each time I do so, it seems that I sink in an inch more into the comfortable zone of blackness. Something profound is going on. I now feel a sense of imbalance. I seem to be tilting and falling in a controlled and predictable way. I follow the sensation calmly with mild interest.

What will happen next? Now there is a sea of white light through which I drift. I cannot tell if it emerges from me or is being absorbed. My breath is suspended, and I watch myself curiously from many angles. I seem to be stretched in every direction in a soft and pleasant way. An aroma of absolute peace moves in and out of my nostrils with no persuasion. I continue to shrink and converge to a point somewhere. I have now burst out with no resistance into a small core within me. Is this the last layer?

Colours dance about, and an understanding pervades this core. This capsule enunciates soft singular syllables of what seems to be Nature in its absolute essence. My eyes close and close again, retreating into this . . . this something. Some layer has been gently removed, and I hear music that I had always known existed but I had never heard consciously.

Let me take you back for a moment to our discussion on pranayama. I spoke about "inhale–halt–exhale" as the process to be repeated in many ways. This understanding of the breath happens when the mind is fully aware of its movement and stoppage.

This analogy comes alive now with a sharp insight.

Recall the concept of samskaras, which are latent impressions retained by the mind over time, spanning lifetimes even. There are numerous such layers of samskaras that need to be erased. Perhaps you have such imprints, too, many of which you wish didn't exist! But try as you might, you find it impossible to erase them!

Patanjali speaks about restraining samskaras and outgoing samskaras.

As the outgoing samskaras attempt to emerge during samadhi, they are held back by other samskaras. This constant internal battle between restraint and expression affects the overall quality of meditation. If the restraining samskaras are not strong enough, your meditation will likely be constantly disturbed. But if they are, the outgoing samskaras will not have much of an effect.

Drawing from the analogy of "inhale–halt–exhale," "halt" corresponds to the restraining samskaras.

During pranayama, I have noticed that the "halt" state is the most potent. Thoughts and discipline are concentrated here. This is where my entire mind and being tends to be focused, between my eyes, even if for a few microseconds. During this time, you may experience intense symmetrical waves of unusual designs, emerging or converging at a single point of focus, which I have written about at the very beginning of this book. At least I have experienced this, and I would not presume that others have not or could not have a similar experience.

Here, too, restraining samskaras serve to subdue outgoing samskaras. This state is the most productive and balanced from a meditation point of view. This could be described as self-control of the highest magnitude.

This is where the mind resembles a gently flowing river with no waves or turbulence. All drops of water move at the same speed, together, in the same direction. There is no "break". There is no barrier in its path.

At this point, the samskaras are well and truly subdued, and there is no possibility of the flow of thoughts being disturbed or distorted.

Samadhi: Singular focus and flow of completely restrained samskaras. All images in the mind along the journey are identical.

This seems an apt place to reproduce an extract of a commentary I once wrote on a great classical raag called Marwa. This raag has a particular hypnotic effect, and expressing it induces a feeling of great tranquillity, not unlike, perhaps, what one might experience in the state of samadhi.

> Marwa!
>
> Deep and grand, mysterious and grave. With rules few can understand and fewer act on.
>
> Do you seek peace and tranquillity in the evening? Do you seek shelter from the heat of Life? Do you crave an existence without turbulence? Do you find wisdom in a rock, waiting patiently for aeons for a reason for its being? Then I, Marwa, command you to sing me.
>
> Marwa! The evening's signature, bidding goodbye to light while preparing for the night. How bold, how indifferent!
>
> The Raag seems to be the source of energy, hinting at secrets and discoveries. See how the water in the lake seems to be less fluid as it moves imperceptibly towards this man sitting by the edge. The trees above

are almost frozen, and the birds on the boughs are silenced by these notes, though the wind blows powerfully, responding to the disturbing challenge of me, Marwa.

Each note within me radiates boldness, power, gravity and understanding. They challenge the mind that seeks self-control. The notes merge with each other without haste, savouring each other.

Meditate. Be still. Let your mind cease to think.

Let your mind cease. Cease.

That is what Patanjali says right up front: Yoga is a cessation of the mind reacting to stimulus.

And now, Patanjali begins a most interesting and subtle commentary, taking off from this point, about the continuity of a fundamental state of mind in a flowing river. The mind keeps mutating through time, sometimes subdued and focused, and sometimes in flux.

Let me start by stating this:

Yesterday's cold ice cube is today's pure liquid and will be tomorrow's hot steam.

How peculiar and how true at the same time!

Here, we see three references to time: the past, the present and the future. We see three states: ice, liquid and steam. We see three descriptors of condition: cold, pure and hot.

We see that we are always referring to the same matter: water.

- The "shape" of water changed: from ice to liquid to steam. This is its dharma, or that which it can become. Water is the underlying common "*dharmin*".
- The "time of existence" changed: from the past to the present to the future. This describes its "*lakshana*".
- The "descriptors" changed: from cold to pure to hot. This is its "*avastha*".

Yet, we agree that we are always referring to the same underlying substrate: water.

Thus, water has the potential to be something else. All it needs are the right conditions.

By extending this logic further, can we say that everything is fundamentally the same and it is only the variation in conditions that makes things look different?

This is electrifying.

Am I not really different from you? Am I not different from any other entity?

This is a crucial question Patanjali is driving at: is the adept yogi capable of physical and mental alchemy?

We shall find out soon.

This is what I gleaned from the first 15 sutras of the Vibhuti Pada:

- When dharana, dhyana and samadhi are progressively and sequentially practised, the action is called samyama.
- The antaranga (internal practices) of one type of samadhi is the bahiranga (external practices) of a higher state of samadhi.
- A material's substrate is the same, but it presents itself differently depending on its function (dharma), state at a time (lakshana) and condition (avastha).

Sutras 16–35

The Vibhuti Pada has been generally considered a very abstract section. But a proper reading makes it clear that it is quite the opposite. It looks at matters from an unusual perspective, that is all, and challenges our assumptions.

The first 15 sutras lay the groundwork. The concept of samyama is presented, and an understanding of several related concepts is laid out. Patanjali gently exposes us to significant new fields of knowledge.

But let us take a step back for just a moment.

As one works with a firm purpose towards attaining perfection or proficiency in any field, new fields of knowledge and abilities open. Not all are rational. Not all are written down in black and white. An expert accumulates knowledge and experiences that a novice does not have. As knowledge increases, additional doorways open.

That is not hard to believe. Electricity would have been considered magic 300 years ago. The Internet would have been difficult to articulate even 50 years ago. But today, many things are taken for granted and explained away as eminently logical and obvious.

Ultimately, what is "rational" depends on your framework of knowledge. You may not know what you do not know. Someone in the jungles of Zambia may not be able to comprehend the concept of snow in Sweden. But someone who has been to both places knows that snow exists.

On a more sombre note, many slaves in Mauritania are

unable to understand the concept of freedom, even today. You, who are likely well-read, may find it difficult to fathom that such ignorance exists.

Just flip it around.

How can you be so sure that certain things are not possible?

Many of us claim to have a "sixth sense"; it may be a momentary acuity of awareness, an unconscious detection of subtle fields of energy or something else. You can often tell if you are being watched. How?

Likewise, then, those who explore yoga with dedication do find an enhancement of sensitivity. This can range from greater awareness of the subtlety of breath, the presence of another person in spirit or even the presence of an "other" entity, specific points of the body, enhanced sensory perception, a feeling of timelessness, greater respect for the immensity of space and so on. I occasionally feel a band of moving currents circling within my head while meditating. That only happens when my asana practice has happened undisturbed, with my full focus on the region between my eyebrows.

Can you feel consciousness? It is not tangible, but it exists.

All this is to introduce the next sequence of sutras that deals with these delicate matters.

We previously spoke of samyama, the sequence of dharana, dhyana and samadhi.

In these sutras, Patanjali proclaims that performing samyama on various objects and their three variables—their function (dharma), their state at a particular time (lakshana) and their condition (avastha)—creates deep awareness of their intrinsic nature and allows us insights into the past and the future.

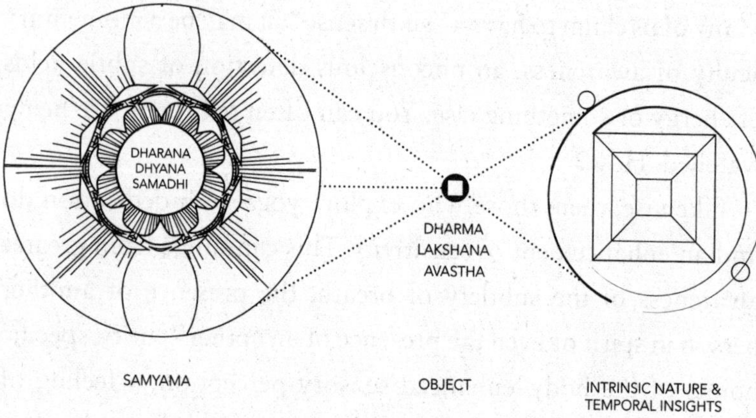

How?

This is not beyond one's capability. Patanjali asserts that if we were to focus on every atomic detail of the object in question through samyama, we would be able to understand their transformation from the past to this point and from this point to the future.

It is just that the mechanics of this process may be unfamiliar and alien to the reader; this does not imply that what has been described is fanciful. It is simply beyond our normal envelope of known knowledge but accessible to the resolute yogi, for whom every second of contemplation brings a new dawn.

Have you noticed that some people have an extremely enhanced ability to learn a language? Within days of being immersed in an unfamiliar environment, they seem to get along quite well in a new set of sonic vibrations that together constitute a new language. Why is that so? Perhaps they have an inherent ability to quickly go down the mosaic of sound and see patterns that others do not as easily.

Here, too, Patanjali asserts that the exercise of samyama that focuses on the difference between words, their meaning and the images they evoke in the mind leads to understanding all the languages of all beings. Sound is only the most obvious aspect of language. It is, in a sense, the outer casing of the true meaning of the word, which is, if you think about it, a certain image that is stored in your mind.

Samyama on a word, its meaning and the image uncover an understanding of all languages.

Patanjali tells us that certain samskaras (latent residual impressions, both active and submerged) spill over into subsequent births. Performing samyama on samskaras creates awareness of one's previous births. If we focus on our attributes, behaviours and contexts, we get a glimpse into what caused them to begin with.

Suspend judgement for a moment and consider that certain people do indeed have enhanced abilities.

Extending this further, if we conduct samyama on the minds of others, we may gain knowledge—and presumably, even control—of their minds.

Is that so difficult to believe? Have we not met people who seem to read minds? Even if it was an accidental trait, that ability does exist—in a sporadic way, perhaps—in certain people.

Performing samyama on people's minds gives us insights into their state of mind at a deeper level than what we do superficially in the normal course, though we may not know why they are the way they are. We may detect a pulse of anxiety, for instance, but we may not know what the person is specifically anxious about.

Remember that we are guided by sensory perceptions about what exists and what does not. The five senses do not explain concepts like "gut feel", an eerie feeling that someone is close by even if they are not, or an ominous, uneasy impression about the impending death of someone we know. We have all experienced this.

Have you not heard about omens and portents? Superstitions, did you say?

And yet, many of us find such matters quite acceptable, even if we find it awkward to express it. It just seems correct.

Patanjali states that when this process set called samyama is focused on the outer sheath of the body, we may become invisible to another.

Scepticism is healthy because we see statements that are orthogonal to our ideas of what constitutes facts. But think about it: the process of sight fundamentally involves capturing the reflection of light from a form. If that reflection is arrested by some means—in this case, samyama—that object is invisible as far as we are concerned. Samyama is in our fundamental physical nature.

Incidentally, there has been considerable research in modern times on the concept of an invisibility cloak. Here, however, we speak of attaining this ability through yogic practices.

We can extend this principle to the other senses (sound, touch, smell and taste), too, and access unusual abilities.

The advanced yogi, with the ability to conduct the process of samyama on whatever he chooses, may also examine karma and arrive at a conclusion about his own death.

Once again, such sporadic abilities are seen in people who foretell their own death with clarity. This is particularly common in individuals considered deeply spiritual. Swami Vivekananda, for instance, supposedly prophesied his death quite accurately.

On the other hand, as an individual, one can have a refined deductive ability to discern the shadow of death on someone else. I know of a person who does possess this ability to some extent. I believe that as he masters samyama, this ability will be honed, not that he wants it necessarily.

We examine the karmic "load" of a person, determine the samskaras created and deduce the likely closure of an existing life.

It must be mentioned in passing that our lore is rich with references to people who possess powers such as invisibility, the ability to foretell death and so on. We brush it off as a charming exaggeration. We think these are fairy tales because they jar with our framework of rationality.

At the same time, it is also true that over time, certain human parameters have changed—we live longer now, but several sensory abilities have diminished. Since we no longer hunt, it can be inferred that acuity in hearing and smell has decreased, which is, in any case, true with routine ageing.

Therefore, at a time when many possessed significant yogic powers, it cannot be ruled out that the powers referred to here, acquired through specific samyamas, were indeed commonplace, or at least generally known.

Extending the discussion, samyama on the feeling of compassion magnifies its radiative intensity. As we push out feelings of envy and malice from within, replacing them with goodwill, the surroundings take on a more positive hue. Again, we have many examples from our cultural heritage that speak of wild animals sleeping peacefully at the feet of meditating individuals in a state of bliss. When an animal sleeps in your presence, it is a statement of great trust because it knows it is completely vulnerable.

This is entirely possible, as we see in our lives. We speak of "vibes" in a positive or negative sense. A malicious person creates a throbbing tension. A good-natured person calms everyone around him.

When I apply samyama to the feeling of compassion, it pulsates around me, softening the sentiments of others.

Samyama on the feeling of compassion (and other positive emotions) is a directed and focused effort to convert potential to action.

By now, you have perhaps started understanding the principle of samyama. If it is directed towards specific goals, specific outcomes result.

Patanjali continues.

If you focus on the strength of an animal (an elephant in the example given by Patanjali), you acquire the strength of the elephant. Recall here that samyama implies taking on the characteristics of the object being focused on. Very specifically, the "alchemic" abilities of the advanced yogi imply the ability to consider the composite of dharma (the fundamental nature), lakshana (the state in time) and avastha (the condition), and pierce through their nature to a fundamental commonality. In this case, acquiring such abilities are well within the realm of possibility.

These prior examples of possibilities prepare us for even

more ambitious explorations. The disciplined yogi can, in effect, understand the nature of objects that may be beyond a normal person's abilities to even fathom. Since samadhi implies accessing the Truth, this ability spreads in all directions, transcending time and space; sensory visibility is the least important in the scheme of things.

Patanjali gives fascinating examples and specifies the implications.

- Samyama on the sun would open the gateway to knowledge about the expanse of the universe and its dimensions. Of course, the universe can be graphically described to include concepts of the seven worlds, including hell and the seven worlds of heaven and perhaps other metaphysically described realms. These are in addition to our normal concepts of stars and planets. The ancient text, *Surya Siddhanta*, contains great details about the movement of the planets.

- Samyama on the moon brings knowledge of the stars. A possible interpretation could be that since emotions are presumably affected by the moon, focusing on the moon gives clarity on how the stars are arranged but even more esoterically, how stars fade in and out like effervescent thoughts.

- Samyama on the North Star, also called the *Dhruv tara* or Pole Star, gives access to how other stars move (and consequently the astrological implications).

- Samyama on the navel brings awareness of every component of the body (not just the physical understanding, but other types of invisible sheaths or pallors that we detect. For example, you might say to someone: "You don't look well" or "You're glowing today!" What has changed? You might know specifically if you could perform samyama on the navel!)

- Samyama on the hollow of the throat causes mastery over the sensations of hunger and thirst. These sensations distract the yogi in his pursuits and must be controlled to the extent possible. There are stories of yogis who have survived for months and years without eating. The late yogi, Prahlad Jani, is supposed to have survived for 76 years without eating or drinking.

- Samyama below the throat of the "invisible" channel called the *kurma nadi*, brings steadiness and stability, both physical and mental. My asana practice has benefitted after I began concentrating on this visualised nadi. It also reduces mental distractions, even if only for short bursts of time.

- Samyama on a particular point on the skull considered to be luminous helps you see evolved entities called *siddhas*, who are advanced yogis and travel across space, time and planes of the universe.

A suggestion for asana enthusiasts: try the kechari mudra involving the tongue pressed against the upper palate while attempting asanas requiring balance. It helps.

Clearly, there are many metaphysical ideas listed above that seem bizarre. However, again, given the mental abilities of advanced practitioners of yoga, these should be considered serious possibilities.

I have personally met people with uncanny abilities, which could not be explained in the frame of rationality that I might have been in. I once met an 85-year-old blind clairvoyant entirely by accident. He accurately described many incidents from my past, including some uncomfortable ones. How? I had never met him before. It was unnerving.

I am sure you have met such people and have been similarly bewildered.

Consider that they were yogis. They just didn't fit the stereotype.

Some of us profess to have great intuition. Patanjali speaks of this as an enhanced ability, which subsumes all the samyama abilities described earlier when at full bloom. This is quite a key point and suggests that a sincere practitioner develops a significantly greater intuitive ability than most.

Most interestingly, Patanjali tells us that samyama on the heart results in a deep understanding of the mind because the heart is where the quality of intelligence resides. There we are: tune your meditative inquiries towards the heart!

These then are three principal lessons I derived from sutras 16 through 35:

- Samyama on various external objects gives us access to other worlds of knowledge.
- Samyama on various parts of the body, too, gives us access and insights into new pools of knowledge.
- A yogi has advanced powers of intuition, in which he possesses all those abilities brought about via samyama.

What I learnt from Sutras 1 through 35 of the Vibhuti Pada

As an aspiring yogi, I am always curious to know what I might discover during my explorations in this ocean.

At its simplest, even doing precisely the same asana every day yields different results or can stimulate muscles you never knew existed. Pranayama is clearly an extraordinary limb of Patanjali's principles, focusing your mind like a magnifying glass on the minutest details of the movement of breath and on how it halts and then resumes.

I experience great peace while practising pranayama after a long session of asanas. I must be doing something right. I am acutely conscious of the need to regulate breath during actual asanas, and this brings with it great peace, reminding me of the sutra in the Sadhana Pada that says that happiness is achieved by stillness.

Not being particularly obsessed or distracted by my senses, except by music (which to me appears to be a beautiful collage of audible vibrations), I can cautiously say that pratyahara is within reach.

It is not that one limb must be mastered before moving on to the next. The sequence is logical on the one hand, but at the same time, it needs to be constantly revisited. It is logical in the sense that these are building blocks and have a natural progression. However, they can never truly be in a state of perfection and need to be endlessly polished. You can never declare yourself to have mastered any limb.

I have found myself more reflective about the yamas and niyamas, while performing asanas practically in slow motion, closely observing my breath.

The composite of dharana, dhyana and samadhi, called samyama, presents a uniquely different challenge. It is not a problem but considers possibilities that are outside the ambit of normal conversation or thought.

Contemplating the possibility that everything is fundamentally the same is quite stunning. Do we indeed possess unusual abilities buried deep inside, waiting to emerge as we confront and admit to this extraordinary proposition?

I do not rule it out. The logical explanation of dharma, lakshana and avastha drives home the point that the substrate of all things is the same. Drilling down further, samyama on anything means deconstructing the triad and, with mental powers sharpened by rigorous practice, rearranging it or uncovering highly sophisticated possibilities.

For almost everything that Patanjali has asserted in this set of sutras, I can claim to have met individuals who have exercised these gifts.

On occasion, I have stared intensely at a specific person in a large crowd and seen them turn in my direction. I have seen the pallor of death on some who seem to be walking about normally, and death has indeed arrived soon for them. To some degree—but sporadically—I can deduce what kind of experiences a person may have gone through in the past to arrive at an explanation of their current condition.

Incidentally, the last erratically visible ability was useful to me some years ago when I used to conduct interviews to hire

MBA graduates. I could identify with a fair degree of accuracy if a person had a hair-trigger temper that might erupt during a crisis or an inability to work in a team. I called it instinct. But was it more?

These are accidental events, no doubt, but they demonstrate that these abilities are possible to discover and hone. And are, I again hasten to add, not unique to me.

I reflect on the intensity of these sutras and the vast range of possibilities they point to. They tell me that great truths reveal themselves to the sincere yogi. And that the more things change, the more they remain the same.

The enlightened yogi may have these abilities at his fingertips but must not engage with them lest he gets carried away. It is merely a great and vivid awakening.

I shall perfect samyama in this lifetime.

I shall change through time and space.

I shall remain the same.

I shall remain changeless.

6

Mastering the Elements

The systematic thinking and progression of ideas of Patanjali may have come across by now. It reflects a brilliant and methodical mind, moving steadily inwards from the world of largely external experiences.

In the Sadhana Pada, for instance, the first five of the eight limbs of yoga were described moving from the outside to the inside, removing layer after layer. In the Vibhuti Pada, Patanjali speaks of the last three limbs starting from dharana and moving into the state of samadhi. Thereafter, there are references to various kinds of samadhi, each more refined than the previous; in effect, going deeper and deeper inwards.

In the prior chapter covering the first 35 sutras of the Vibhuti Pada, Patanjali spends time explaining how samyama (the process of dharana, dhyana and samadhi as a unit) works on external matters, moving inwards to the heart. This kind of samyama brings some significant abilities to light, some that may be considered impossible to believe. However, be assured that one may move from a state of incredulity in relation to a claim to finding it quite believable.

One such example is the 17th sutra that alludes to sound and language, which says that samyama on the difference between a word, its meaning and the image it invokes in your mind results in understanding all languages.

Sutras 36–45

Moving on and in the same vein, Patanjali says samyama helps to differentiate between intelligence (*buddhi*) and the true self, referred to as purusha.

Much has already been written about how the seer tends to identify itself with the seen, the ego being the facilitating culprit.

Samyama on the sattvic intelligence reflects the pure image of purusha. Why sattvic? When rajas and tamas are truly suppressed, the mind is entirely balanced and in harmony (sattvic) and is at its purest.

With such purity come two enhanced abilities—the power of intuition and the five sensory perceptions. That is interesting and worth our consideration.

With sattvic intelligence comes heightened intuition and enhanced sensory perceptions.

Intuition implies clarity of practically everything, which seems logical at this stage in this stream of discussion.

Enhanced sensory perceptions also make sense, yet they stand in contradiction to the idea that the mind must not be swayed by sensory distractions that beckon the rajas and tamas gunas.

This is the point: that the mind is so pure that the highest of sensory distortions are not to be engaged with.

In other words, while they may be superficially great attainments of the pure mind, they also serve as the last test for the yogi in the state of samadhi. We can assume that they serve as a stern reminder of that which is to be discarded. You will see more of that in the Kaivalya Pada.

Again, it is not hard to relate it to day-to-day experiences. Whoever attains excellence or perfection in anything is likely to develop additional critical abilities consequently. However, engaging with them excessively is a mistake. For instance, a resolute musician may develop an ultra-fine ability to discern very minute errors that most others cannot. He may make the mistake of allowing his ego to distract him by engaging with his own genius, thus missing the whole point.

What does a centrifuge do? It separates various components of a fluid. As it spins at great speeds, contaminants or denser material separate and move outwards, leaving behind something pure and lighter. That is also the principle of a butter churn, which separates thick butter from buttermilk.

In a similar fashion, the denser powers separate out from a yogi during the process of samyama but are not to be confused with the pure "material" left behind.

It is easy to be taken by the spiritual butter—the "powers", but the real essence is what the true yogi seeks.

Once this stern ability to dissociate heightened sensory perceptions from the mind occurs, the mind is separated from the body and can become a freewheeling entity, so to say. The body's sensory abilities seem irrelevant and comical and not worth any attention. By extension, the mind can move from body to body.

Hold that thought!

There are many stories in our lore of this ability of exalted yogis to exit their own body, enter another body and return.

In a well-known example, the great saint and philosopher Adi Shankaracharya was locked in a debate with another brilliant scholar, Madana Mishra. Shankaracharya had established his proficiency over practically all areas of knowledge, except that of conjugal intimacy, which he had hitherto not been interested in and had no experience in as he was a *brahmachari*, a celibate.

As this deficiency in knowledge came forth during the debate, Shankaracharya relinquished his own (physical) body temporarily. He then entered the body of a king who had just slipped into death, surrounded by his wailing queen and other courtiers. To the shock of onlookers, the king came alive with absolute vigour, resumed his daily life, and subsequently learned the art of lovemaking over a period of time.

However, the queen of the (newly alive) king noticed a distinct change in his persona. So did the ministers. He seemed wiser, thoughtful and altogether different. There was great suspicion that some other exalted person was in the king's body.

In any case, after several weeks, Shankaracharya returned to his original body, armed with his newfound knowledge, and proceeded to win the debate with Madana Mishra.

The original, fascinating story can be investigated in greater detail elsewhere.

Such stories in our cultural heritage are more common than you might imagine and give cause to reflect.

In this instance, we could argue that the power to exit one's body and enter others demonstrates with clarity that the body is fundamentally irrelevant. If this power is to be exercised, as

Shankaracharya did, then it needs to be for the rarest of rare purposes.

Patanjali's subsequent discussions of levitation would therefore not come as a surprise; if the mind can enter and exit bodies, the power of levitation is relatively easier to understand. He refers to a particular *pranic* force, the *udana*, as something an adept yogi can harness to accomplish levitation.

The warning is, of course, that these are not for display, entertainment or any other nefarious purpose. It exists as a capability for the pure mind to be used rarely, if ever.

A true yogi can exit his body and enter another and also has the gift of levitation.

Another esoteric principle is mentioned by Patanjali—the *prana*. Four "subsidiary" pranas are listed: *samana, apana, vyana* and udana. These are "life-forces" with specific functions, including the distribution and release of energies. At the time of death, the main prana exits from the top of the head and all other pranas cease functioning as well. The chart below summarises the principle:

1 Prana Intake			
2 Samana	**3 Apana**	**4 Vyana**	**5 Udana**
Distribution, assimilation	Downward, elimination	Circulation	Ascension, upward

The adept yogi has additional proficiency over the five pranas and can therefore use them as needed. There are even instances of individuals bursting into flames at will when they decided it was time to relinquish their bodies.

You may find that incredible.

However, you would most likely agree with me if I were to state that some people have a radiant aura. What makes them stand out in a crowd? Why do we automatically turn towards someone in a gathering? What is so special about them that they have established a presence despite not having uttered a word?

Patanjali states that this is due to an understanding of the samana prana. Of course, we are referring to the adept, but the example was to illustrate how the principle manifests.

All these powers exist, either dormant, intermittently used (without awareness) or with full awareness.

Proficiency over the pranas gives unusual abilities to the yogi, including self-combustion and unusual radiance.

Nevertheless, if you are prepared to defer to the possibility of these powers being available to the expert yogi, who is no longer attached to his body yet uses its potential in other ways, it would not be hard to imagine that a yogi can take sensory perceptions to quite another level.

If the normal human ear can scientifically hear 20 Hertz

(cycles per second) to 20,000 Hertz, imagine what the yogi would potentially hear if he conducted samyama on the interface of the ear with ether (space)!

Outer space is filled with unusual sounds; where did they originate from? What is their purpose?

Could the intent of these sounds be clear to the yogi?

Of course, sound is only one aspect. Taste, sight, touch and smell are likely to be considerably enhanced in a comparable manner, accessing experiences that are out of the question for a non-yogi, and are probably impossible to comprehend by most.

Patanjali's exposition carries forward in a few subsequent lines:

- Samyama on the difference between the body and ether and focusing on the lightness of cotton helps you travel in the air.

- The yogi is capable of out-of-body experiences. Well, if he can exit his body and re-enter it later, as mentioned earlier, this capability seems prosaic! The reader has probably heard about out-of-body experiences. Again, this is in line with the thinking that the pure mind is indifferent to the body and can dissociate with it.

Samyama on various sensory interfaces can enhance hearing, aid the yogi in flying, and lead to out-of-body experiences.

Once again, notice the outside-in quality of communication

and revelations. Patanjali has taken care to ensure that his points are understood by speaking of tangible matters and getting you ready for other more complex revelations as he removes layer after layer. This is an overarching theme noticed across various sections of the Yoga Sutras.

Here is an example that you can probably relate to:

> Query: What are the five acknowledged elements?
> Response: Earth, Water, Fire, Air and Ether.

You could hardly argue with this statement of fact, and you are likely to understand it without much trouble.

Let us look at the sequence from "most subtle" to "most gross".

1. Ether (space) transforms into air.

2. Air transforms into fire.

3. Fire transforms into water.

4. Water transforms into earth.

The interconnectedness implies, therefore, that every element has some component of all the others!

How do we move from subtle to gross? What does it mean? Let's see.

Can you hold ether? No.

Can you hold air? No. But in a balloon that you could hold, yes.

Can you hold fire? No, you would be burnt, but it feels

vaguely tangible—you can see the flames and sense the heat.

Can you hold water? Yes, though we see that it takes the shape of its container.

Can you hold earth? Yes. Definitely.

The next graphic illustrates how gross elements contain within them subtler elements.

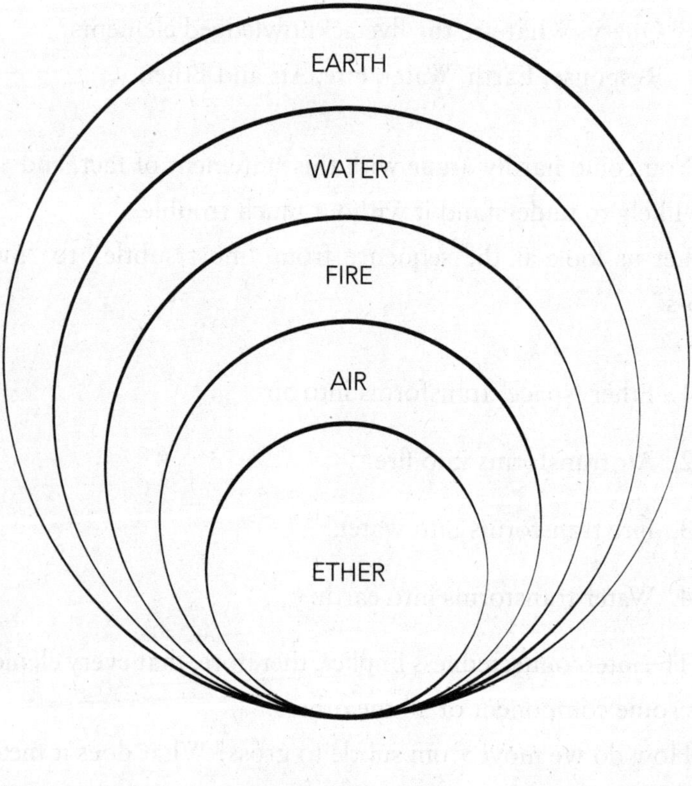

Your mind is now ready for the next set of principles. Patanjali moves further inwards.

Query: What attributes do each of them possess?

Response: Their manifestations, essential nature, subtle nature, how they relate to the others and their purpose.

The next graphic conveys the essence of what Patanjali wishes to convey: by performing samyama on the five attributes of each element, you gain mastery over it.

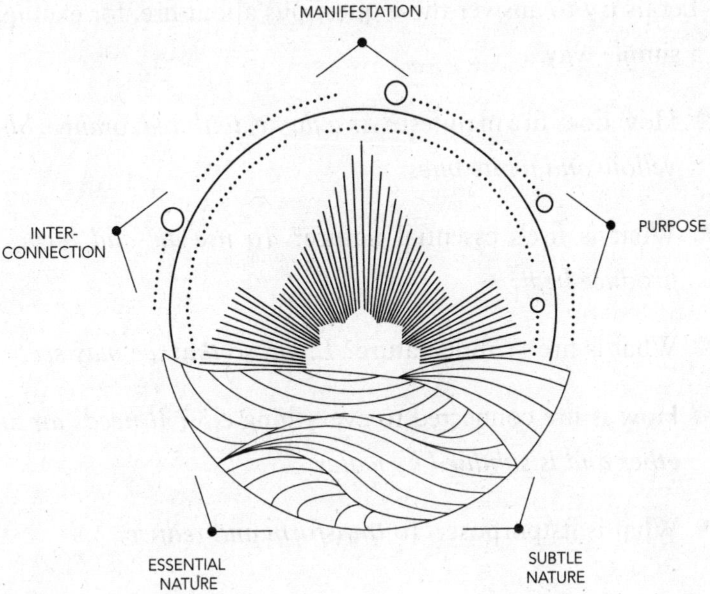

At first sight, this may seem a little challenging. That need not be the case. But first, let's try to deconstruct.

An element's subtle nature is sensed through a sense organ.

- The earth (the element) is sensed through smell (the subtle nature) and through the nose (the sense organ).
- Water is sensed through taste through the tongue.
- Fire is first sensed as light through our eyes and then as heat.

- Air is sensed through touch through the skin.
- Ether is sensed through sound through our ears.

Let us try to answer these questions about fire, for example, in a simple way.

- How does fire manifest? *As a flame, with red, orange, blue, yellow and white hues.*
- What is fire's essential nature? *To use air and burn, to produce heat.*
- What is fire's subtle nature? *Light, so that we may see.*
- How is fire connected to everything else? *It needs air and ether and is subdued by water.*
- What is its purpose? *To transform and reduce.*

We can do a similar analysis for the other four elements.

Patanjali states that conducting samyama on these questions for each element results in mastery over them.

Samyama on the elements and their attributes helps the yogi master them.

How does this knowledge manifest in the yogi?

Patanjali asserts that the body can dominate the elements and has no limitation per se.

This is easily expressed thus:

- Fire cannot burn the yogi
- The Earth yields to the yogi
- Water slides off the yogi (like oil)
- Wind does not apply force to the yogi
- Ether, otherwise not seen, now covers the yogi and makes him invisible.

Such is the power of focused samyama that the elements yield their secrets and allow themselves to be dominated.

In the same penetrating and highly charged sutra, Patanjali alludes to the extraordinary powers that a yogi possesses in relation to these elements.

- Minimisation—shrinking to an atom
- Weightlessness
- Maximisation of weight
- The ability to gain anything at all
- No constraint on the will to do something

- Control over all the elements
- Changing the external appearance of anything
- Altering the elements as desired

This (partial) list of powers is certainly mind-boggling. Not because they seem fantastic. No, by now, we should have acknowledged that the power of samyama is quite intense, especially when we do so on the elements.

But this list is quite a revelation. Sceptics would certainly find this beyond the pale of reason, but once again, we must also admit that most of us have limited pools of knowledge due to circumstances, exposure, knowledge and fundamental intelligence and can hardly be expected to fathom the powers of a yogi. It is best to withhold judgement.

Previously, we have spoken of the fact that the mere ability to have certain powers does not justify using them. Two points emerge:

- These powers are a by-product of attaining something rarefied through the practice of samyama. The true yogi is indifferent to those powers. They are to be used in the most unusual of circumstances. Our lore does speak of exalted individuals exercising these powers—becoming infinitely small, large or invisible or being untouched by fire, etc. The story of Vamana growing to a colossal height and placing his foot on Bali is one such tale.
- The yogi who is entranced by the powers that he now

possesses risks going astray and may end up defeating the very purpose of samadhi.

These sutras are a nuclear physicist's dream! Going down to the atomic level and understanding the nature of elements and what the possibilities are—well, Patanjali seems to have been a person of infinite intelligence and insight!

These then are my learnings from the study of these sutras:

- Samyama on pure intelligence reflects the purusha—with that comes enhanced intuition and five sensory perceptions.

- Once the mind is free of the irrelevant body, it can move between bodies. Other powers like levitation, enhanced hearing, out-of-body experiences and so forth become possible.

- The yogi can master the elements like fire, water, earth, air and ether. He can change physical attributes and manipulate elements in the manner he chooses. These powers are incidental, and a true yogi ought to exercise them in the rarest of rare circumstances.

Sutras 46–56

The preceding sections delve deep into areas that may be considered esoteric and mysterious. Samyama is clearly something that is acquired with intense and relentless practice. Once the process is fundamentally understood, mastered, and internalised, the adept yogi shifts the target of samyama and acquires capabilities that defy ordinary reason.

Once again, the brilliant communication strategy of Patanjali is seen. Moving progressively from the tangible to the intangible and even the almost incomprehensible, he prepares the readers for additional forays into the mind of an expert yogi, whose body, he says, epitomises graceful perfection "like a thunderbolt, with the brilliance of a diamond" and so on.

This is a not-so-subtle reminder that the yogi would reach this exploration of samyama only after perfecting his body's capabilities. The body and mind are now at their rarefied peak.

Now Patanjali moves to even subtler levels to explain the possibilities that exist.

We have previously spoken of Pratyahara, the fifth limb of the practice of yoga, which deals with the withdrawal of the senses (which we take as essential because they prove to be endless sources of distraction). An even finer explanation would be that no matter how fine your senses are, you choose not to engage with them.

The senses, he says, can be analysed across five levels via samyama.

- What is their natural state? What do they sense?
- Why is this sense needed? What if you didn't have this sense? By extension, is there a sense we don't have?
- What is the need of the ego to use the senses? The ego misleads and proclaims: "It is I who am sensing."
- How do the three gunas—sattva, rajas and tamas—manifest via the senses?
- What is their purpose in relation to the perfect purusha?

Analyse the senses: their natural state, the reason for being, their impact on the mind, triggering the gunas and their ultimate purpose with respect to the purusha.

When these questions are thoroughly analysed (through samyama), mastery over the senses is achieved; they reduce to insignificant distractions.

Notice the progressive movement from the outside (the senses themselves) to the deepest understanding of their necessity in the context of final perfection.

Now, therefore, when the senses have been "reduced" to their basics in the manner described, Patanjali says that several powers are "released" from their bondage. These include an extreme speed of thinking, movement independent of the body and dominance over natural elements.

Stories abound of divine entities spontaneously manifesting in front of people who seek favours. While superficially amusing, we now see that they hint at the five-stage mastery and understanding of the senses, as so beautifully described by Patanjali. It is interesting that our culture easily accepts these "appearances"; clearly, the imprints of thousands of years of acquaintance with individuals possessing such abilities through generational storytelling cannot be dismissed.

Free of the senses, the yogi becomes independent of the body.

As the shackles of the senses are shaken away due to the revelations brought on by samyama, the last strands of the bond between the seer (purusha) and the seen (prakriti) are finally broken. The gunas, while fully understood, lose their potency, and instead aid the explanation of the past and future and knowledge of space. In short, the yogi, as a perfect purusha, has unlimited power and pervades all dimensions.

But the probing continues. Patanjali does not stop here and demands more of the one who seeks. Indifference to the attainment of this supreme knowledge is the prerequisite to ultimate liberation. One might say, in a convoluted, recursive way, that awareness of the need to be indifferent to awareness is the final goal.

This, previously referred to as asamprajnata samadhi, is also known as kaivalya, which is expanded beautifully in the fourth section of the Yoga Sutras.

Patanjali then sounds a note of caution. But in preparation, let's talk for a moment about the process of gaining proficiency in music.

In stage 1, the student explores music. Mistakes are made and corrected. Perfections appear in irregular ways. There's plenty of labour, excitement and frustration. Improvement is incremental, and an impatient student may give up the battle.

In stage 2, the student has reached a thrilling state of proficiency. He receives praise and acknowledgement from family and friends and becomes eager to show the world what he knows. He may develop an ego and may wish to start performing. The world offers temptations in the form of money and recognition. Most students are easily swayed at this stage and may even consider continuous practice as an annoying though necessary distraction.

In stage 3, for a more serious student, the quest for perfection and deeper insight continues. He realises that social recognition is fundamentally silly and without merit and acts as a distraction in the personal pursuit of deep knowledge of music.

In stage 4, the student transcends his own identity, merges with music, and becomes impervious to anything at all.

Drawing upon this analogy, Patanjali warns the yogi that it is easy to regress and stray. The journey is long and strenuous. At a certain stage, as the yogi starts becoming firm in his resolve, he will be tempted by various spirits with promises of pleasure, just as a budding musician feels the need to perform in public before he is truly ready. If the yogi ignores these temptations, his journey will continue uninterrupted.

References to celestial entities are seen in several texts. To most people, this appears irrational. But that is only because "modern education" teaches us to consider irrational anything that cannot be experienced, seen, documented, repeated and so on. And yet, traditional societies worldwide are quite accepting of the existence of spirits and do not find such acceptance incongruous.

You will find references to spirits in the traditions of Native Americans, the aboriginals of Australia, many tribes of Africa, the Maoris of New Zealand, in the ancient culture of Egypt and so on. There is nothing unusual about it. It is merely the "modern man" who has been told that such concepts do not bear scientific scrutiny and must be dismissed as superstition.

In our context, celestial entities may seek to thwart a serious yogi who seeks to perfect his knowledge. Once he remains razor-focused, he will attain a stable and enjoyable state.

The yogi may be swayed at exactly the time his latent powers start manifesting.

As the universe becomes attainable in all dimensions, including time, Patanjali exhorts the yogi to perform samyama on the smallest possible unit of time.

The concept of time is at once intuitively understood as well as impossible to fully describe. Is it a clumsy human contrivance needed for practical purposes?

We use time to explain the shifting nature of experiences. We also observe that we cannot recreate past moments. We think the past, present and future cannot exist at the same moment.

But when the yogi conducts samyama on the smallest unit of time, his discriminative awareness becomes acute.

What is the smallest unit of time, then? Traditionally, it is called "*anu*". And since we cannot truly grasp time, we need to look at it differently. We exist in the moment; we do not exist in the past or the future, though it pleases our ego to think so.

Conducting samyama on these moments in infinitely small points of succession is what gives us acute discriminative intelligence.

A yogi with this precisely defined discriminative intelligence can detect the difference between two objects. These objects may appear identical in every way but are different in one precise way—their atomic arrangement!

We have difficulty in distinguishing identical twins, though the mother can. It becomes increasingly difficult to separate the two as we go deeper and deeper into finer and finer identical objects.

Take two grains of rice. They may look identical in shape, colour, weight and even length. You could not tell the difference between the two under normal circumstances. But the yogi with discriminative power achieved through samyama on the smallest unit of time and its successive moments can do so!

This ultra-fine discriminative ability can be "exploded" into a metaphysical understanding of the past, present and future intent of all objects. This way, the yogi does not view time as a sequence at all. Indeed, the past, present and future coexist!

And if so, this is a liberating idea because it spans births and deaths and explains the intent of all objects.

Why does a mosquito exist? Of what use are various species of fish deep underwater, like the Mariana Snailfish that lives 8,000 metres below sea level? Why do metals exist? Why are there so many species of butterflies?

What is the purpose of the universe? Where did it originate? What is its true size?

The answers to these imponderables—and an uncountable many more—are instantly available to the adept who has reached this state of discriminative intelligence after samyama on the smallest unit of time.

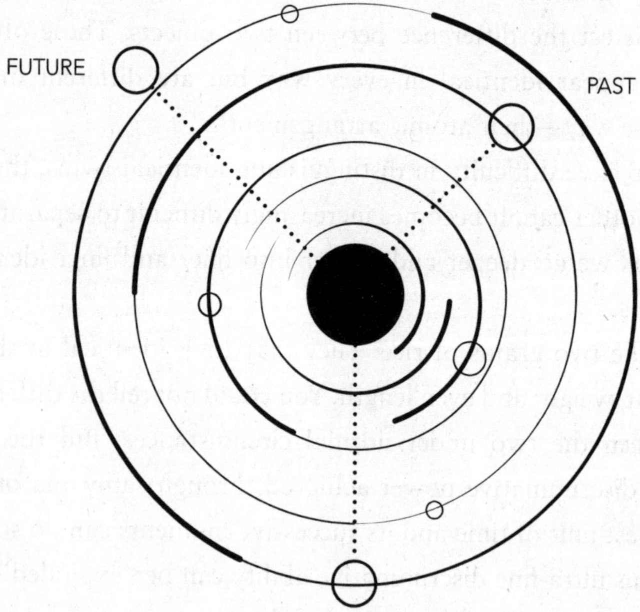

Now, rid of all imperfections, casting aside rajas and tamas, devoid of kleshas, fully aware of all knowledge and yet indifferent to it—the yogi attains liberation! More of this in the upcoming Kaivalya Pada!

These then are my learnings from the last set of sutras of the Vibhuti Pada:

- Samyama on the senses liberates the yogi and achieves movement independent of the body, among other things.

- The yogi must be aware of the possibility of being distracted when he achieves a level of proficiency and must be on his guard.

- Samyama on the smallest unit of time gives discriminative intelligence and provides us with a clear understanding of the purpose of all things across space, time and form.

What I learnt from Sutras 36 through 56 of the Vibhuti Pada

It is possible to go through an entire lifetime merely existing, consuming oxygen and never really appreciating life's meaning or pondering its purpose.

It is possible to merely scratch the surface of the immense amount of potential that lies within. A misdirected, empty life. What a sad waste!

I cannot claim to be substantially different. I have been buffeted by the winds of life, just like anyone else. I have been swayed by pointless distractions and been completely consumed by rajasic and tamasic impulses.

But along the way, I have resolved, from time to time, to return to sanity and develop a yogi's perspective of what life is all about. It has been a classic case of two steps forward and one step back (or even many steps back!). I have been ordinary and accept that I may not develop perceptibly in this lifetime.

Going through the phenomenally interesting Vibhuti Pada gave me insights into possibilities that only a single-minded focus on understanding yoga might reveal.

The messages in this specific set from the Vibhuti Pada (sutras 36–56) must be understood as a whole and not necessarily in sequence.

Let me start by speaking of discriminative intelligence acquired through the process of samyama.

It seems clear that brilliant insights require the mind to be sattvic, i.e., when it is balanced and calm. Though pratyahara urges the withdrawal of the senses, it is interesting that understanding and applying the process of samyama to various senses serve to amplify them in multiple ways. Sattvic intelligence gives heightened intuition and sensory perception, which in turn are to be considered irrelevant for the larger purpose of yoga.

On a side note, much has been written about depriving the body of nourishment to cause the brain to function faster.

"The faculties become refined when you starve them," the mythical detective Sherlock Holmes once explained to Watson in the story *The Adventure of the Mazarin Stone*. "As a doctor . . . you must admit that what your digestion gains in the way of blood supply is so much lost to the brain."

He continues in the same vein: "I am a brain, Watson. The rest of me is a mere appendage."

Was Holmes a different kind of yogi?

I digress.

Weakening the sensory faculties consciously through pratyahara serves to enhance them through the process of samyama!

But this then is an acid test—would this enhancement cause the yogi to "stray"?

I think these matters of self-control are quite applicable. I am now acutely conscious of sensory perceptions because I watch them react and apply restraints.

Let's say there's a delicious aroma in the air. Under normal circumstances, I might salivate. But now, especially after a meditative session, I might ask, "So what? Be indifferent."

This is a significant milestone in my overall progression,

slow though it may be!

Other kinds of potential powers such as exiting the body or even levitation may come along; who knows? I know this as a possibility after reading the sutras, but at the same time, they hold no allure for me. That is very likely the intent anyway!

I am quite aware that right after a meditative session, with complete awareness of the flow and distribution of air through my body, the cells of my body relax and radiate contentment. A sceptic may say it is imagination. It might well be. Nevertheless, the sensation exists, and I do feel the experience. Therefore, for me, it is real.

As a musician, I have been long aware that certain sequences of notes or even an extended single note can be meditated upon. I repeat them often, as a kind of samyama, and they express themselves differently every time. When I meditate in such a manner, they shift in a certain way and release a story that is impossible to articulate. They seem like little windows that open into another dark, pulsating welcoming universe, pregnant with secrets.

There is now a greater awareness of the elements. I ask questions to no one in particular: what is the purpose of this element? As I meditate further, sometimes there are glimmers of understanding. That is enough to keep me going.

And now that I am urged to perform samyama on time, I hope to gain an increasingly greater understanding of the reason why anything and everything exists. I would like to believe that the past, present and future will perhaps merge, and I would have clarity about the meaning of everything. I do understand this may take years, if not lifetimes, to accomplish. However, if time itself is fundamentally merely a sequence of existential states, the issue of births and deaths ought not to matter.

It is clear then that one must master the eight limbs of yoga, learn the process of samyama and bow before Patanjali to say:

I know nothing.

And in doing so, perhaps one day in some lifetime, I might say:

I will know everything.

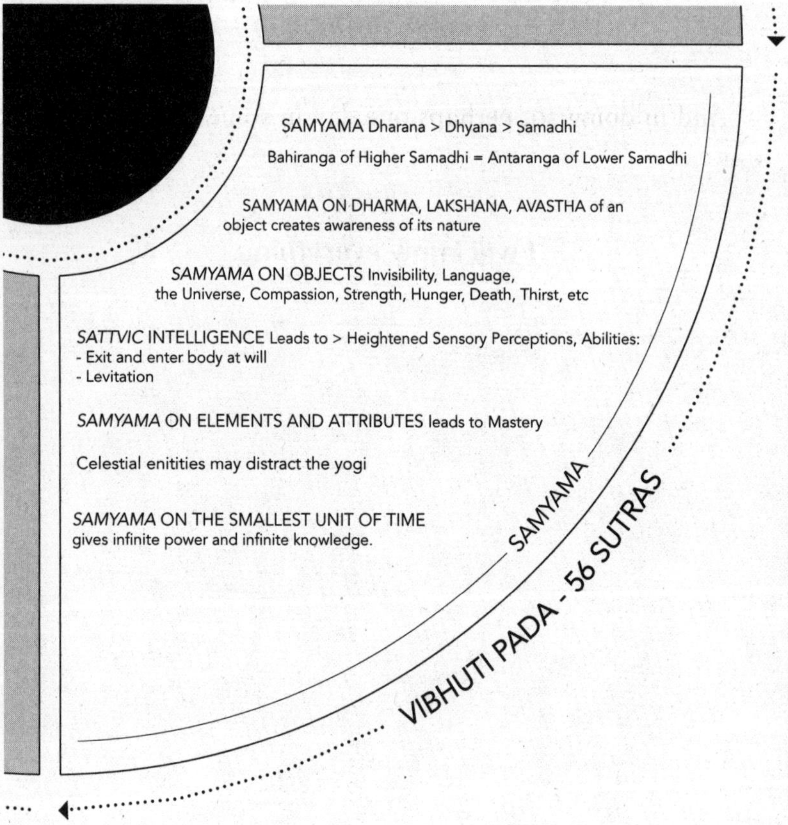
SAMYAMA Dharana > Dhyana > Samadhi
Bahiranga of Higher Samadhi = Antaranga of Lower Samadhi
SAMYAMA ON DHARMA, LAKSHANA, AVASTHA of an object creates awareness of its nature
SAMYAMA ON OBJECTS Invisibility, Language, the Universe, Compassion, Strength, Hunger, Death, Thirst, etc
SATTVIC INTELLIGENCE Leads to > Heightened Sensory Perceptions, Abilities:
- Exit and enter body at will
- Levitation
SAMYAMA ON ELEMENTS AND ATTRIBUTES leads to Mastery
Celestial enitities may distract the yogi
SAMYAMA ON THE SMALLEST UNIT OF TIME gives infinite power and infinite knowledge.
SAMYAMA
VIBHUTI PADA - 56 SUTRAS

Section 4

The Isolation—Kaivalya Pada

7

The Path to Convergence

Traversing the Yoga Sutras a sutra at a time is a blissful and intense experience.

New possibilities spring up, and beautiful concepts take shape. After the first pause, when confronted with an unfamiliar concept, the idea you see expressed seems so vibrant with a feeling of "truth".

Patanjali's ability to explain complex paradigms comes across in many ways—through repetition, paraphrasing, structuring and so on. There are no loose ends, and no axiomatic statements are left to our imagination; everything is laid out clearly. The power of the mind with its pulsating energy is presented to us in multiple dimensions.

Having first laid out the meaning of samadhi, Patanjali then moves on to explain how to achieve that vision in the Sadhana Pada, with a specific focus on the first five limbs (yama, niyama, asana, pranayama and pratyahara), which largely looks at the external experiences that need to be understood and mastered.

And then, in the Vibhuti Pada, he explains what happens when the three final limbs—dharana, dhyana and samadhi—work in concert as the process of samyama, "unleashing" dormant powers that threaten to sway the yogi. Managing these mystic powers firmly and even being entirely indifferent to them is the decisive test for a yogi, as it were. Through the dedicated and sincere practice of samyama, you acquire powers that you can use in the rarest of rare cases.

Sutras 1–17

In the concluding section, called the Kaivalya Pada, Patanjali starts by explaining that these extraordinary powers, extracted through intense, sustained meditation, can also be derived from other means:

- Through birth, presumably, as one of the last ones of a yogi, going up through refined stages of samadhi
- Through herbs, which trigger certain reactions and give you a "push"
- Through the chanting of certain mantras, which create frequencies and harmonics that act as catalysts
- Through austerity, which has been explained in some detail before, but which bears repeating; minimalism and actively pushing away sensory bliss, which focuses the mind and opens channels

Birth, medicinal herbs, chanting of mantras, austerity and meditation: these are the vehicles to acquire extraordinary powers.

Shedding samskaras and karmic "baggage" may take a few cycles of births and deaths, so the first point is easily understood. At some point, the yogi takes his final birth, with all his practices and dedication converging to this period.

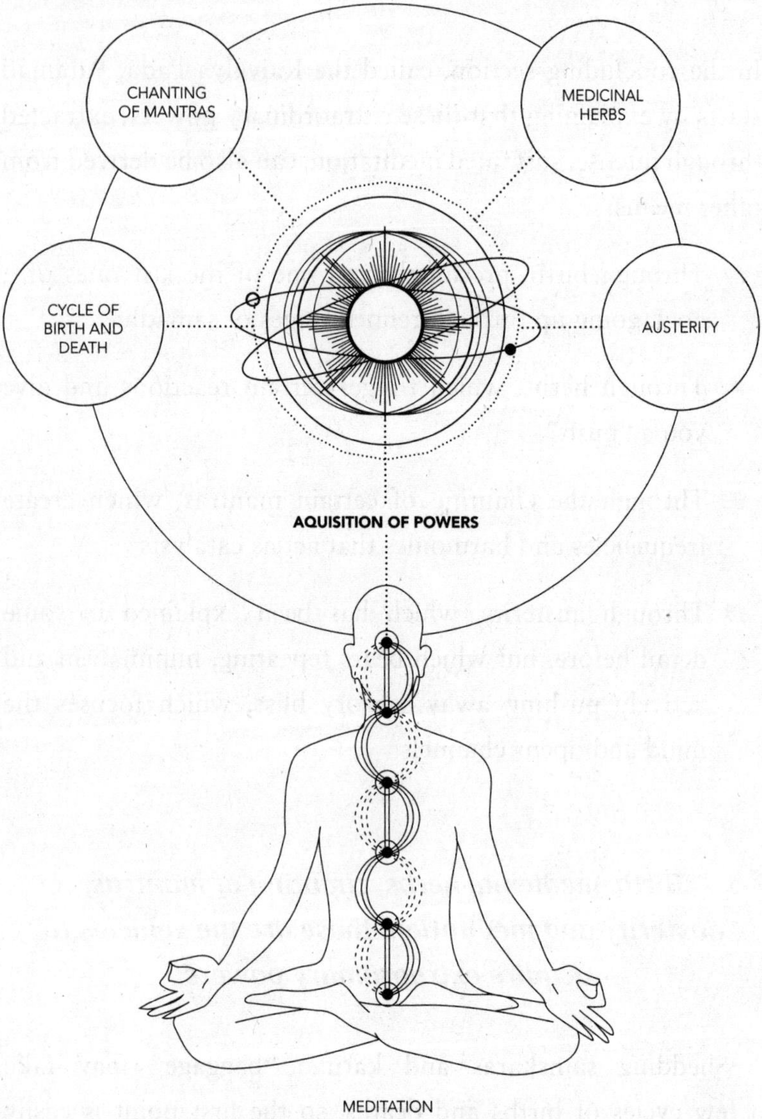
CHANTING
OF MANTRAS
MEDICINAL
HERBS
CYCLE OF
BIRTH AND
DEATH
AUSTERITY
AQUISITION OF POWERS
MEDITATION

The references to mantras and austerity are also understood, as their practice brings one-pointedness in effort and intent. When everything else is blocked out, the determined yogi is bound to make geometric progress using these aids.

The point of herbs can be easily misunderstood, however. Is Patanjali suggesting using drugs to attain powers?

Not really.

Of course, we know that mind-altering drugs do exist in various cultures.

For example, in certain countries in South America, a herbal brew called ayahuasca is recognised and accepted as part of religious ceremonies. In some parts of Africa, a hallucinogenic shrub called iboga is used as part of an elaborate ceremony to connect with spirits. Peyote, a small cactus that contains psychoactive alkaloids, is common in Native American communities in their ceremonies.

In India, many social groups see no challenge in using natural herbal drugs like *bhang (ganja,* cannabis) to get into a state of mind that fosters its opening to spiritual experiences. The Atharva Veda (*Kanda 2 Sukta 2 Mantra Sankhya 5*) specifically mentions cannabis as a sacred plant with healing properties.

Though social codes today frown on such practices, it cannot be denied that these are more a norm than an exception for many people seeking spiritual experiences.

Our beautiful stories speak of *sanjeevani* as the herb that gives life. Specifically, Hanuman was tasked to bring sanjeevani to the battlefield in Lanka to heal Lakshmana. Moreover, bhang is routinely consumed during the Hindu festivals of Holi and

Shivratri. It is, therefore, not odd for Patanjali to have explicitly mentioned this.

On the other hand, since I have no personal experience in the matter, I could not say if this is a good idea in modern circumstances due to the possibility of other synthetically created drugs being mixed. In addition, many drugs do harm the body after the initial "high"; caution is therefore advised.

In sum, Patanjali says that though meditation is the ideal means for a yogi to acquire extraordinary powers, which he must be indifferent to, other methods exist to accelerate the process.

As we move along, Patanjali changes gears very subtly and addresses the issue of rebirth.

Are humans expected to be born as humans again?

Not necessarily, he says, deflating us a little as we have been brainwashed that the human form is somehow at the apex of everything. We have self-certified our superiority.

Nature—prakriti—decides in what form a rebirth is necessary, keeping in mind the karmic fruition that is necessary. Perhaps as a goat, perhaps as a worm, perhaps as something else. Consciousness pervades the universe and is present in everything that possesses life. Yes, even that Mariana Snailfish that lives 8,000 metres below the surface of the sea!

Recall that the kleshas (remember them? Ignorance, egoism, attachment, aversion and the fear of death) and samskaras carry forward and embed themselves in the mind (*citta*). These need to be resolved in some manner in some necessary life form.

In the Vibhuti Pada, Patanjali speaks of the yogi, who, through samyama, understands why anything and everything exists. Thus, a goat or a worm or a human form has a reason for being and may be considered as a perfectly logical receptacle for someone going through a cycle of birth and death in a specific way. Nothing is an accident. Every life form is equally important in the grand scheme of the universe.

All living beings have a reason for existing. You may be reborn in a non-human form, depending on the nature of your karmic baggage.

I remember my late mother warning me that even the accidental killing of a worm might result in me being reborn as a worm. Far-fetched, you might say, but given my (new) appreciation for how all things work in concert, I find it an authentic possibility. If this consciousness permeates animals, then harming or killing them is quite the same as harming myself!

Ahimsa is intended to be the predominant driver of our behaviour, both internal and external; most have failed, myself included. Therefore, there is every possibility that I have created enough karmic material through my actions over many lifetimes to be reborn in the most appropriate form, which may not be human!

I disagree with the notion that the power to reason separates us from other animals, who we think act purely on instinct. There are many examples of collective intelligence. Migratory birds, baby turtles, ants, bees—they are guided by instincts that we do not possess. They may possess intellect of an entirely different kind. Their reasoning may be of a different kind that we have not understood (and therefore presume does not exist or is irrelevant). You will not find malice, envy, possessiveness, greed and other traits in them—all of which we struggle to shrug off during our lifetimes. So, where does that place us?

Tangentially, I find it remarkable that these allusions and hints of how everything works have come down through generations as part of oral cultural traditions. It is easy to admire oneself as being extremely intelligent, modern, progressive and rational and dismiss these age-old beliefs as superstitions. However, many of these matters definitely have more than a hint of being rooted in truth.

Now, back to rebirth.

With clear insights into prakriti's possibilities, the yogi works to remove obstacles toward emancipation. If obstacles emerge and are not removed, rebirth continues, with the citta inhabiting various forms in different births. The adept yogi, like a farmer channelling water, removes barriers and allows the free, uninhibited flow of nature, moving closer and closer to the final, pure state of yoga.

Can a single mind exist in only one body? The question is not strange; in fact, the idealised pure mind, bereft of ego, does not cling to a specific form. Recall that in the Vibhuti Pada, it was mentioned that the mind can shake off the physical body and wander anywhere it chooses.

As an extension, then, Patanjali proclaims that the yogi can exist simultaneously in multiple bodies.

This is a mind-bending notion (pun not intended).

Be that as it may, the core, extremely subtle point is that an individual mind is ultimately the creation of the ego! Therefore, consciousness must be all-pervasive and not be limited to a single form!

As the mind blends into consciousness, it can create multiple strands of thoughts, like the tendrils of a vine. As indicated earlier, the perfect mind can exist simultaneously in multiple forms, all controlled by one "master" mind that exercises its abilities to withdraw them into itself.

These are powerful concepts that can cause us to pause and wonder if we are separate and distinct (as we might like to believe because it suits our sense of vanity) or an extension of someone else's mind!

A few sections prior, we referred to the story of Shankaracharya exercising his yogic powers and existing simultaneously in two physical states—his own and that of a king. Perhaps he was in a state of suspended animation in one and in active animation in the other while maintaining a connection between both!

The mind of a yogi can exist in multiple entities.

Returning then to the theme of the perfect mind, which Patanjali refers to at the beginning of the Kaivalya Pada, there is only one among the five types of minds that is untainted in any way—and that is the one born out of meditation. Despite exhibiting powers referred to in the previous Vibhuti Pada, the rest still have a karmic "stain". Meditation subdues and destroys the kleshas and does not generate any karmic fruits. There will be no action due to samskaras either.

Patanjali takes a moment to describe the nature of karma of a yogi, which is not difficult to follow if you recall a previous discussion on the nature of gunas.

The first type of karma is "good" (sattvic, white), the second is "bad" (tamasic, black), and the third is a mix (rajasic, grey). Clearly, any individual is likely to generate various combinations based on their actions, which are sometimes very pure in intent, very negative in intent or a mixture of good and bad intent.

But the practised yogi is beyond that. He is indifferent and does not create any karmic action, even while indulging in necessary action. He has no desire and is not concerned with the fruits at all. The first three types of karma obviously create impressions, while the last does not.

Karma, driven by intent, can be bad, good or a mixture. In the case of a yogi, it is colourless as it is not driven by intent.

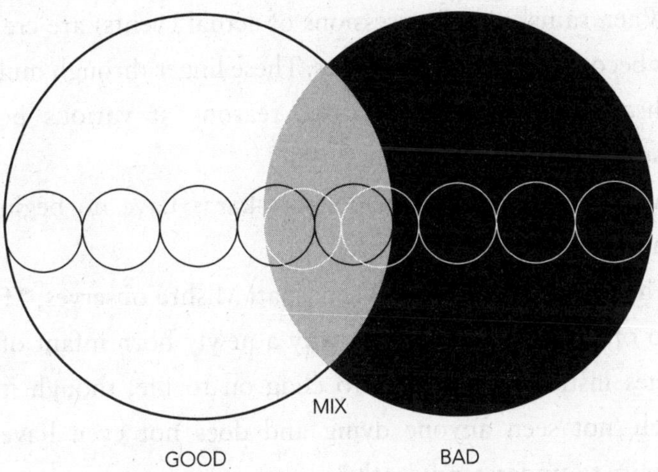

KARMA DRIVEN BY INTENT
(NON-YOGI)

Shades of the Bhagavad Gita!
Krishna says in Chapter 5:

"... devotion through action is better than renunciation. He is an ascetic who seeks nothing and rejects nothing..."

As a result of filling our cup through our lives with the first three types of karma, subsequent lives will see them bear fruit. Not necessarily in the very next one, but perhaps later, triggered by the right circumstances. But clearly, when the master yogi can ensure that no further karma—good or bad—is added to the "collection", the process begins of breaking the cycle of birth and death.

When samskaras (impressions of actual events) are created, they become, in effect, memories. These linger through multiple births, activated due to karmic reasons at various points, irrespective of place, birth and time.

A profound point is made: samskaras have no beginning because we seek to live forever.

The great commentator Vachaspati Mishra observes, “There is no other explanation as to why a newly born infant of any species instinctively wishes to cling on to life, though it has clearly not seen anyone dying and does not even have the capacity to understand death.”

This point is important for a yogi—how does he transcend the fear of death to break free and attain eternal liberation?

Why and how do samskaras persist? Patanjali states that these are supported by:

- Step One: The cause, which creates the desire for an experience.

“I wish to drive a Mercedes-Benz, and I don’t care how I get to do so. I’ll do anything!”

- Step Two: The fruit, which is the result of the sated experience.

“That was an amazing drive! What a car! I may have stolen a car to get that thrill, but so what? Hey, life is all about living on the edge!”

- Step Three: The underlying layer of karmic collections to which the new experience is added.

"I have now added the experience of driving a stolen Mercedes to my karmic bank balance."

- Step Four: A provocative object that reminds one of a particular experience, which stimulates the samskaras that were waiting for a signal in the current lifetime or much later.

"Oh, look! A new Mercedes! I can't forget that thrill when I stole a Mercedes in a previous birth a hundred years ago and zoomed through town! I ought to try it again!"

This stimulation is thus once again the cause; we return to Step One, and the cycle completes and starts again.

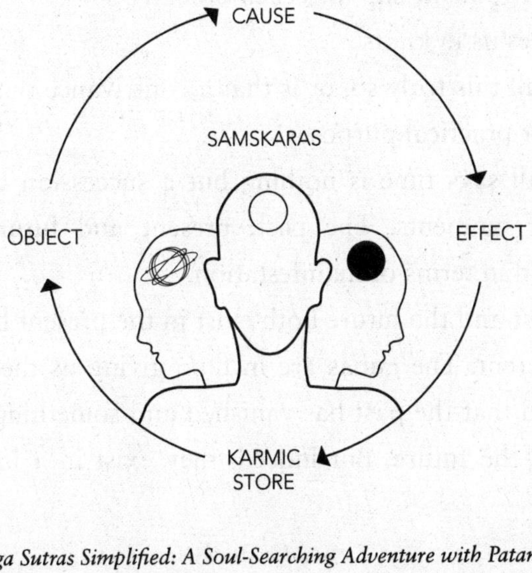

Samskaras persist because of cause, effect, the store of karma and the object that triggers the samskaras. The cycle continues till identified and broken.

Once the yogi recognises this vicious cycle, he can apply discrimination to identify specific elements of the cycle, weaken them and then be free. Samskaras are now no longer created.

Patanjali spends a great deal of effort on the analysis of time. He did so in the Vibhuti Pada, and he does so again here.

We are consumed by the concept of time. We think of the past. We think we live in the present. We anticipate the future and plan for it. We regret the time wasted. Sometimes we wish that time would accelerate when we look forward to seeing someone. Moments slip into each other.

Time ties us in knots.

But is all this truly so, or is that a contrivance that we have created for practical purposes?

Patanjali says time is nothing but a succession or flowing stream of moments. The past, present and future can be understood in terms of manifestation.

The past and the future both exist in the present but merely seem different. The gunas are in flux, giving us the mistaken impression that the past has vanished and something new will emerge in the future. But indeed, they exist in a latent form in the present. As the balance of the gunas keeps shifting, from manifesting to becoming latent, so too does our clumsy perception of past, present and future. In the end, the objects in question are the same but are perceived differently because of the constant churn of the gunas.

The yogi understands these alterations and is unaffected by them. The seer observes the seen blanketed by gunas and is indifferent. The ego is erased.

If an object exists, does it present itself similarly to multiple minds? The answer is no. For instance, one person perceives a dog as a friendly, harmless and pleasant animal. Yet another perceives the same dog as dangerous and is terrified by just looking at it. Why?

Once again, as in the previous case, it is merely the interplay between the three gunas that causes this distortion. Each person is influenced by a different combination of the gunas and reacts differently.

The unending disequilibrium of the gunas (sattva, rajas and tamas) causes us to perceive objects differently or reinforces the concept of past, present and future.

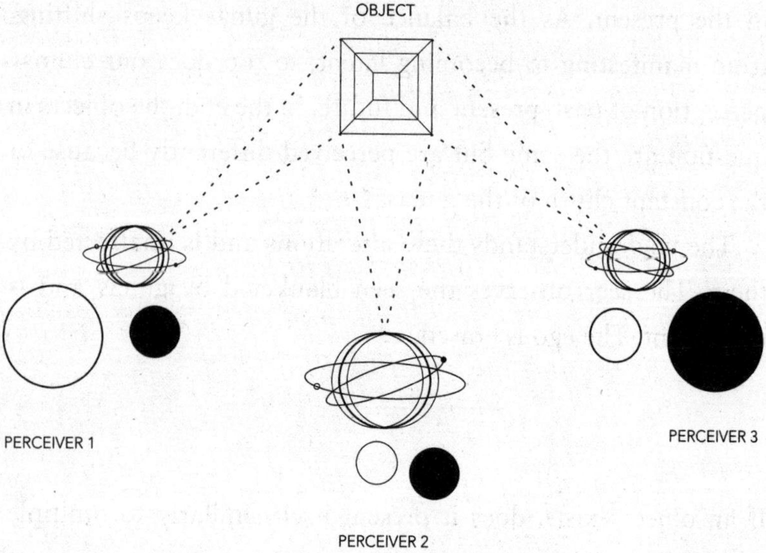

This, of course, leads to another question. If a mind—any mind—does not perceive an object at all, does the object exist in the first place? If the object fails to stimulate a mind, is it, in effect, invisible or non-existent?

A similar philosophical point was made in the not-so-distant past by Charles Riborg Mann and George Ransom Twiss in the book *Physics*, "If a tree falls in a forest and no one is around to hear it, does it make a sound?"

Thus, if a mind notices an object, it is known. If it does not, it is not known.

Extend this idea to many minds.

If the known object is looked at through the prism of expectation, it takes on a certain hue. If there is no expectation, it reveals its true nature.

This is the refined, most subtle state of the mind that

considers time and objects through the shifting sands of gunas. This mind, when completely unaffected, sees their universal truth as one entire whole.

These were my lessons from assimilating the first 17 sutras of the Kaivalya Pada:

- There are three types of karma–black, white and grey. All are driven by a motive. The last, exhibited by the true yogi, is one in which he is not concerned with the fruits.
- Samskaras are a function of cause, effect, karmic "collections", and the object that stimulates the samskaras.
- The past, present and future coexist and are considered distinct merely because of how they are perceived due to shifts in the gunas; in fact, they are one.

A yogi speaks through the mystical Raag Ramkali, known to induce elevated thoughts:

> "I know that everything must end, but the gift of life must be respected. Your experience must be clean, sinless and pure.

"Step away from attachment while being rooted in the world. Watch your parents age, watch your children go, watch wealth appear and disappear. Never feel sad about these things but participate nevertheless, because to be detached from those who too must exist is to be a coward.

"The harsh word evaporates before it forms in your mind. Violence transforms into gentleness and love. Lies disappear, and humility reigns. Hate will have no meaning, and revenge will seem pointless. You will see Purusha in the poor and sick and serve them without the expectation of reward or recognition. This is the beautiful purity of me, Raag Ramkali."

What I learnt from Sutras 1 through 17 of the Kaivalya Pada

So effortlessly subtle and yet precise, Patanjali's pronouncements are crystal clear in what they seek to convey. But our own shortcomings and lack of intellectual depth may prevent us from absorbing the lesson in the first instance. A couple of additional perusals may be needed, and we could still fall short of grasping what is strikingly obvious and yet elusive at the same time!

After navigating the bottomless and vast ocean that constitutes the remarkable concept of yoga, the Kaivalya Pada starts the process of convergence.

I was momentarily distracted by the very first sutra that speaks of spiritual accomplishments. There is a reference to the delicate area of special herbs to trigger spiritual experiences that result in the acquisition of mystical powers, which are referred to in the Vibhuti Pada. That is one way. Other ways exist that appealed to me, including austerity and meditation.

In any case, I also looked at my own reaction to that point—did it underline a certain prejudice? Did my upbringing and conditioning make me react the way I did—with confusion and scepticism?

After a lifetime of pointless distractions and "living in the present", entirely helpless in the currents of kleshas and the three gunas—am I asking a lot to wish for spiritual liberation? These rarefied and pure ideas need years of single-minded focus or at least an elevated level of self-awareness to absorb.

Nevertheless, I am at least knowledgeable now about the direction in which to go and have the necessary advice from Patanjali.

Endless digressions and distractions are possible, but "as a farmer removes obstacles between fields for the flow of water", I, too, shall now be aware of what stops me from moving forward.

Being aware that the mind can potentially exist simultaneously in multiple forms is an intriguing feeling and lends itself to a new perspective of thinking. Empathy comes to mind—why does that person feel the way he feels, which is quite different from what I feel? Should I now understand that the other person's mind and my mind are in fact part of the same fabric but just happen to be subject to a different mental and physical environment?

So far-fetched and so obvious at the same time!

Similarly, do my dogs and I share a common mind?

Karma explained! If I do something with deliberate intent, I am bound to the consequence. If the effect was good, I shall retain that memory and repeat it under the right conditions. I shall be chained by my samskaras and be bound to a karmic destiny.

Motivated by something, we create karma, good or bad or a mixture. But a true yogi, I now understand, performs actions without a specific desire for gratification. Again, the striking image of Krishna advising Arjuna on the battlefield comes to mind.

"Act without wishing for the fruits."

How simple, how profound, and yet—so difficult! If karma is produced, the fruits will expend themselves over lifetimes while being constantly refreshed by additional karma provoked by samskaras.

What must I do to stop this endless cycle? When did it even begin?

Once I capture the cycle of cause, effect, karmic residues and stimulating objects, I can hope for release.

Another profound philosophical foray was triggered by Patanjali's observation about the concepts of past, present and future existing only because of the shifting quicksand and relative intensities of the gunas. Does this mean that the way we understand time is fundamentally flawed?

So, in effect, the three gunas weave continuously about us, spinning a tale that creates illusions. One involves that of time presenting itself as past, present and future. On the contrary, time is a "liquid" stream of moments where the past, present and future coexist. Likewise, objects are not modified in their perception—they are simply clouded by new, ever-fluid veils derived from combinations of gunas. That seems to be the last constraining concept.

This, too, explains why what I see as perfectly logical may appear illogical to another. The object's neutrality is hidden because we have not (yet) developed the yogi's sense of acute discernment.

And flipping it around, and sending me into another philosophical tailspin, is the idea that an object exists irrespective of who perceives it. Does it cease to exist if it is not perceived because of a mismatch in expectations?

I see that Patanjali has taken a comprehensive view of the concepts of time and karma. Once we understand time, as he hopes we will, everything makes complete sense.

What then am I? Merely a karma producer? A developing yogi?

I exist if you think I do.

I do not exist if you think I do not.

Time describes itself as a vision to a yogi:

> "Surrender completely to me," said this indescribable apparition. "I am formless, faceless. No one can capture me; no one can control me. My shadow falls on everything and everyone, and escape is impossible. I have watched the Universe from when it was the tiniest speck of dust.
>
> "I move neither forward nor backwards like the rest of you trapped in my relentless current. I shall

witness countless births and deaths but shall not grieve. I shall witness beauty and sordid decay but shall not be moved by either.

"Desperate to halt the passage of time, you grieve for more to experience. But time will consume you in the end. You are nothing. You have been touched by me and are helpless.

"Your hair greys and your skin withers. Panic is useless. You grieve for a lost moment, you long for the smile of your lover. But nothing endures.

"Nothing."

8

The Brilliance of Solitude

Gently probing, explaining, amplifying—Patanjali, as a tour guide of the complexities of existence, has been exemplary. The attention to fine detail and sophisticated analysis, challenging our ability to grasp the point, has been breathtaking. Patanjali has proven to be a remarkable communicator, holding our attention throughout.

Sutras 18–34

In the Samadhi Pada, he referred to purusha, which we understand clearly as pure consciousness. The purusha is unchanging and eternal, immune to change.

As we continue with the final set of sutras that constitute the Kaivalya Pada, going deep into the mind and nudging us into the direction of supreme isolation, we are reminded that it is the seer—the purusha—watching the gyrations of the hysterical mind (citta).

Recall the very first line of the Yoga Sutras that says that yoga is the stilling of the mind. Purusha, pure consciousness, like a deep and still lake, watches the mind's struggles as it reacts to constant bombardments through the five lenses (again described early in the Samadhi Pada).

Thus, the seer observes the mind and comments neutrally on its state of complexity at that time. Am I agitated? Am I feeling happy? Am I anxious?

Who is "I"?

The "I" here refers to the seer, and the descriptor ("anxious", "agitated", "happy") is the state of mind. Expressing this in a different way, the mind cannot comment on its own state; it is the object of analysis.

Patanjali affirms—and it seems axiomatic at this stage—that the purusha is all-knowing and self-aware. The mind is not self-aware but is aware of objects. It perceives and senses.

Let's think about it.

Self-awareness (a quality of the purusha) and object-awareness (a quality of the mind, citta) are distinct concepts that cannot be discerned simultaneously.

Further, Patanjali affirms that the mind can only be one—you cannot possess more than one mind! If you did, you would be in a constant state of confusion.

This is challenging to comprehend in the first instance but starkly logical in the next!

I cannot exist with multiple cittas! It may be that you feel your mind is in a terrible flux, overflowing with wildly fluctuating moods and thoughts, and extremely disturbed. You may even say, "I am in two minds", which is merely a figure of speech.

But finally, it is only one mind, with only one set of memories, that is a receptacle for samskaras. It is only one mind that is perturbed by the five kinds of modifications (spoken of right at the beginning of the Samadhi Pada) and the five kleshas.

It is not obvious. It is a deep and profound point. We are given one mind and cannot switch or swap minds on demand. Imagine the confusion if we had more than one mind! What thoughts would bubble up? What kinds of contradictory signals would we be unable to resolve? Would we have two sets of conflicting memories?

Do not confuse this with the psychological condition called Multiple Personality Disorder. There, too, we have only one mind but demonstrate different shades at different times.

What we are talking about is not a matter of a single mind displaying more than one set of characteristics at the same time.

In our case, we mean one mind. The one that processes stimuli, the one that we are trying to subdue, the one that is constantly accumulating samskaras. Your mind.

You cannot have multiple minds.
You can have only one.

Purusha, while passive, is completely aware of itself by reflecting off the mind. As the mind changes, the purusha merely marks the reflection as a lake with ripples might imperfectly reflect the moon at night. While the mind is subject to constant change, which the yogi is repeatedly exhorted to control, the purusha is not; it merely observes without reacting.

The moon is still, but its reflection is not. Do not imagine that the moon is rippling! It does not and cannot change!

The mind observes the external world through sense objects and constantly mutates. In turn, it is observed by the purusha, which remains unaffected. If the mind were to be still, it would reflect the purusha perfectly.

From a distance, you may not be able to distinguish between the real moon and the moon reflected in the still lake!

Thus, for instance, I—through my eyes—observe a beautiful landscape. My mind is affected, and a sense of pleasure pervades. But I, as an observer, merely record and note this change in my mind.

And taking that idea further, the restless mind, with numerous imprinted samskaras, exists solely for the purusha.

Recall a similar idea elsewhere: the seen exists for the seer!

I am reminded of something I wrote in the context of describing a classical Raag Purabi Kalyan, which creates a meditative ambience:

> The hold of Shadaj is too strong for the one whose mind wavers, who is distracted by the beauty of the moon outside, whose entire purpose is exactly that—to sway and disrupt the focused mind. And when

one refuses to be swayed, the moon shows itself as something else, the reflection of God's soul.

The mind takes in sensory inputs, dips into samskaras or creates them, and keeps building and rebuilding itself. It clearly does not exist for itself. It is for the unchanging purusha.

This distinction, initially difficult to comprehend, now makes sense. It is no longer necessary to dwell on the question of identity. The issue of "I" is now understood.

At this point, when the mind, with profound discriminative awareness, realises its distinctiveness from the purusha, the yogi has a "Eureka moment" and automatically accelerates towards liberation!

When the mind realises its distinctiveness from the purusha, the yogi moves towards liberation.

It does not follow, Patanjali warns gently, that once in this "post-eureka" state, liberation is automatic and without hindrance. Some samskaras may still be imploding and disintegrating and may continue to make their presence felt, though perhaps with less intensity. This implies that the feeling of being unique and distinctive may linger on in the yogi's mind, no matter how advanced. We simply must be aware that this is likely to be the case and be watchful.

Fair warning!

But the ideal yogi, fully aware that these disturbances

potentially exist, and armed now with the power of acute discriminative clarity, can brush them aside as a minor nuisance. Remember a prior discussion about how kleshas (products of the experience of living) are also weakened and ineffective. The same principle applies now to residual samskaras that no longer have the power to derail the advanced yogi. They sublimate into nothingness.

Kleshas and samskaras become irrelevant.

One of the highly refined thoughts that recur in Patanjali's discourse is of a yogi's indifference. Elsewhere, the yogi was exhorted to be dispassionate. Very specifically, he was warned that great "magical" powers would emerge and that he should not be swayed. Indeed, he must be indifferent to these powers. If not, he would be sucked back into the world and may have to start his endeavours all over again.

Likewise, Patanjali says that the yogi, at this stage, has acquired significant, indescribable knowledge because of finely honed discriminative intelligence. As a result, samskaras no longer have the power to influence.

The yogi must be indifferent to even this highly exalted comprehensive knowledge and may even consider it a nuisance!

I know that I know—and it does not matter any more!

This ultimate state of indifference born out of advanced meditation is referred to beautifully as dharma-megha samadhi, which translates approximately to "the samadhi of a cloud of virtues".

The cloud has burst, washing away everything, even knowledge. The yogi is now a shining, radiant, liberated flame drenched in a profound mist of knowledge that he is indifferent to!

The body is irrelevant. Knowledge, too, is irrelevant. The mind (citta) is still, and the purusha is soaked in self-awareness of the highest order. This is true nirbija samadhi.

Concepts like kleshas and karma self-destruct and no longer have any relevance.

At this stage, knowledge is irrelevant.

What a glorious picture!

An exalted yogi, in serene solitude, his mind expanding and entirely self-aware, untouched by the karmas and kleshas that countless others battle with through lifetimes ... a delightful and awe-inspiring image!

The yogi is liberated and is no longer subject to the notion of rebirth.

The yogi, drenched in the rains of true knowledge, knows everything that truly needs to be known. There is little of relevance that remains to be understood. Sensory perceptions no longer bring forth anything resembling new knowledge.

It follows that the gunas are no longer relevant. The whole wildly fluctuating cocktail mix of sattva, rajas and tamas disappears for the yogi. Their purpose has been served as the mind is stilled. The yogi no longer cares for "experience".

Time, as described earlier, is nothing but a ceaseless stream of moments. The gunas ultimately cause us to differentiate one moment from another, giving rise to practical concepts like past, present and future. All objects change imperceptibly through the sequence of moments as the gunas keep morphing.

The average person observes change over a period. The yogi observes change at the tiniest unit of time, the moment, as if he were taking a photograph of the object.

The meaning of time is fully grasped.

We now have a situation where the yogi, untouched by the gunas, is now able to fully grasp the concept of time and is simultaneously indifferent to it!

He stands alone, in the profound state of kaivalya.

Time, space and place—all are now irrelevant to the yogi, drenched in the rains from the clouds of virtue.

Patanjali takes a moment to remind us that the goals of man over the duration of his lifetime are four:

- One: dharma, which translates roughly to duty on every dimension.
- Two: artha, which refers to the acquisition of enough material objects or money to sustain the needs of man in his quest for liberation. (Such a practical point!)
- Three: kama, which refers to the pleasures of life, inasmuch as one must become aware of one's body as part of the journey and look after it with care.
- Four: moksha, which refers to liberation.

The gunas are necessary to progress towards these goals.

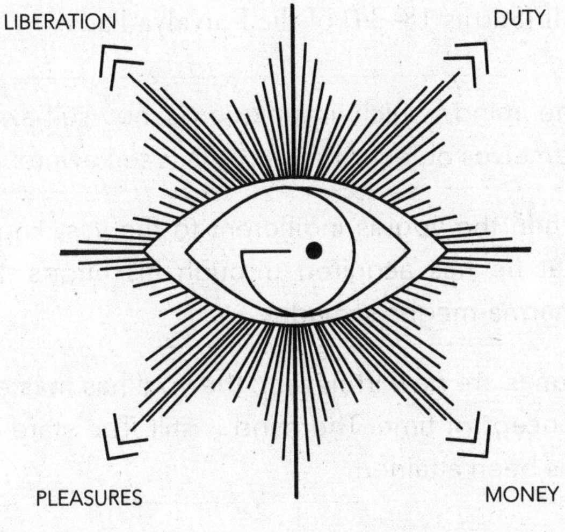

A MAN SEEKS

Now, at this stage, however, the yogi has discarded the gunas, which served to provoke and challenge through the act of creating experiences and fulfilling karmic obligations. The goal has been reached. The mind (citta) no longer reflects worldly turbulences, and the purusha is back in its own essential nature.

The mind has been stilled.

The objective has been achieved. The yogi has merged with purusha.

The yogi is in a state of brilliant, perfect solitude.

Kaivalya.

"And this is it," says Patanjali and puts down his pen.

These then are the three lessons I received from the profound second half (Sutras 18–34) of the Kaivalya Pada:

- The mind, which is unique, is not self-aware but perceives objects; the purusha is self-aware.
- When the yogi is indifferent to the vast knowledge that he has acquired through his efforts, he is in dharma-megha samadhi.
- Gunas are now irrelevant; the yogi has mastered the concept of time. The mind is still. The state of yoga has been attained.

What I learnt from Sutras 18 through 34 of the Kaivalya Pada

The last set of sutras in the Kaivalya Pada, which mark the end of the entire text, is refined and supremely elegant. I felt—rather dramatically, I do accept—that Patanjali was sitting in front of me and pointing towards an extraordinary conclusion. Abstractions were resolved, a great convergence was explained, and a few gentle final warnings were given.

Let me say this in succession: "I was angry". "I am sad". "I shall be happy."

In these three sentences, I have captured states of mind and time.

And I have also referred to "I".

This sense of identity is now clarified.

My mind—*citta*—will soon realise, I hope, that it is distinct from that sense of identity. Through arduous study and practice of the multiple limbs of yoga, perhaps I shall inch closer to that sense of separateness.

And I have also been exposed to a remarkable reinterpretation of time. It is, I now understand, an approximation of the idea that appeals to us, that we understand in some manner, that there is a past, there is a present, and we believe there is a future. But given our knowledge of how everything comes together, we see that all objects are fundamentally the same but appear to change because of the endless juggling of gunas.

Further, though seemingly obvious, the point is made that only one mind exists and that having multiple minds is an impossibility. Patanjali challenges or clarifies even the most obvious point by explaining why it is so. This description helps!

On reflection, I realise that I may have felt lonely at various points in my life. In the absence of a mental anchor, I felt I was suspended in space, which stretched endlessly in all directions around me. But I see now that there is a remarkable beauty in such a singular suspension.

"Lonely" is a word contrived by a coloured view from a sense of ego. But we are all indeed alone, and there need not be any fear or sorrow associated with that state. And in the final, sublime state of kaivalya, it is of utmost aspirational value.

In a short story that I had once published many years ago, this little paragraph described this "suspension":

> I dangle in a space of infinite depth below me. How odd it is, that my very individuality persists, and others have not subsumed me. Indeed, we do not need to persist or even be absorbed. Time and other norms do not apply. There is no one to please, no one to answer to. There are no expectations. Time and its shadow do not touch us.

And what better way to imagine oneself than in that beautifully evocative phrase: dharma-megha samadhi. Even saying it aloud is moving.

It brought a feeling of infinite bliss to my mind, as though someone had gained access to another ocean of impossible-to-describe knowledge, which I might choose to ignore completely. Knowledge that renders our current existence, this body, and this set of experiences entirely irrelevant. The kleshas, the karmic load I carry, the subliminal samskaras—all must be rendered pointless in the last mile, inching closer to purusha.

The true meaning of time will perhaps reveal itself to me.

I pray to Patanjali that my long journey, either of this life or the next one, will end in kaivalya.

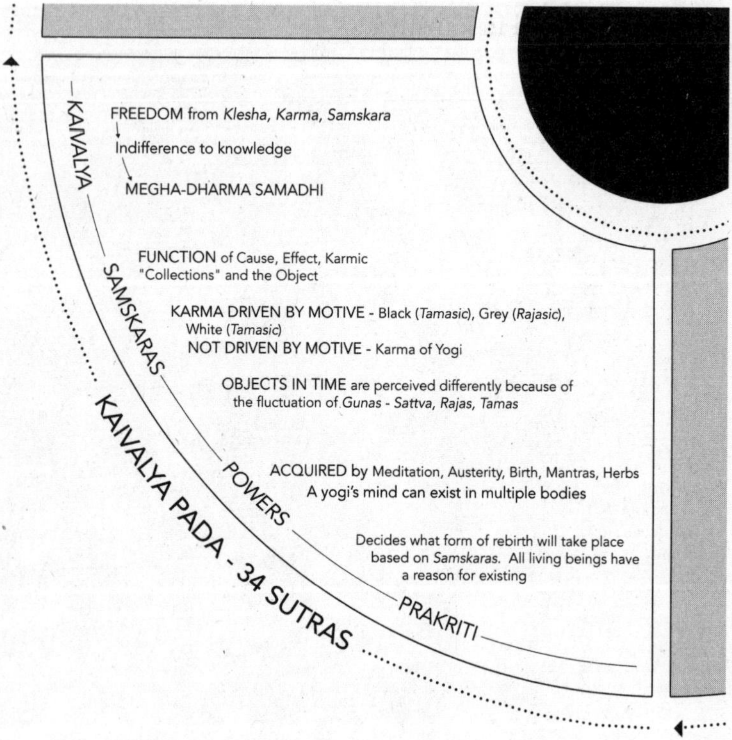

KAIVALYA PADA - 34 SUTRAS
KAIVALYA
FREEDOM from *Klesha, Karma, Samskara*
Indifference to knowledge
MEGHA-DHARMA SAMADHI
SAMSKARAS
FUNCTION of Cause, Effect, Karmic "Collections" and the Object
KARMA DRIVEN BY MOTIVE - Black (*Tamasic*), Grey (*Rajasic*), White (*Tamasic*)
NOT DRIVEN BY MOTIVE - Karma of Yogi
OBJECTS IN TIME are perceived differently because of the fluctuation of *Gunas - Sattva, Rajas, Tamas*
POWERS
ACQUIRED by Meditation, Austerity, Birth, Mantras, Herbs
A yogi's mind can exist in multiple bodies
PRAKRITI
Decides what form of rebirth will take place based on *Samskaras.* All living beings have a reason for existing

Distilling the Yoga Sutras

Trying to unravel a majestic, timeless piece of intellectual expression is effectively futile, even if stimulating to the extreme. I was left mentally drained several times as I studied the Yoga Sutras, trying to understand the original lines and looking at the formal interpretations of several scholars, who often differed in the intent and purpose.

Patanjali, as a master communicator, gets straight to the point. He says that an enlightened individual must understand that the mind must be made impervious to stimulation. The quivering jelly must transform into an impregnable diamond. And once that happens, we will merge into that pure consciousness that pervades the universe infinitely in all directions.

But alas, that is easier said than done, sighs Patanjali. Let me explain, he says.

He goes on to describe the evanescent mind and what makes it behave arbitrarily. He speaks of five types of provocations. Once you recognise them and subdue them, you will see your true nature.

Deep inside is the real you, clouded by the rust of so many things. Brush away the rust and dust.

But it's never easy, is it? The rather weak and insipid nature of human existence is acknowledged by Patanjali. Illnesses, sloth and more contribute to providing distractions. They give us an excuse to stop the attempt to still the mind. But when did you even start, asks Patanjali, and urges us to develop positive feelings and learn to meditate.

Meditation.

Yes, it's not easy; no, not at all. A troubled soul at work, a deeply depressed young teenager, a repressed and lonely adult—how do we ask them to meditate? "The deeply searing moments of anguish are just so real and personal," they say. "And you want me to meditate? Even if I do, would that make my problems go away?"

Patanjali does tell us about the way in the beautiful Sadhana Pada. But he prefaces it towards the end of the Samadhi Pada by explaining the overall process and stages. This is an invaluable aid and gives us direction and hope.

Meditation is difficult. Very difficult. Initial attempts are always frustrating. Monks sitting in a cross-legged pose radiating peace, as seen in pictures, seem impossible to imitate. How do they do that, we ask. Are they just posing for photos?

"My mind is constantly on the move; I'm helpless! How in the world do I meditate?" you ask.

Unfortunately, there is no shortcut. The stages described by Patanjali are a good and easy-to-understand way to go about the process. Take an external object and dwell on it for a few seconds a day, gradually increasing the number of seconds. Merge with it. Observe the senses and then move within. The process continues; Patanjali has described it beautifully. It seems futile to attempt describing it in quite the same manner. But finally, Patanjali observes that the quieter mind dwells on the light within and finds great peace.

Yes, a day will come when you feel a thrill of satisfaction that you meditated!

Communication

There's no point in being very intelligent if you can't communicate.

Let me speak of one of the two overriding communication techniques used by Patanjali to get his point across.

The first is of describing the goal and then working backwards. Patanjali breaks it up thus:

"This is samadhi, and this is why it's necessary."

"This is how you go about achieving it."

"There are a few risks, but the benefits outweigh them. The powers you may acquire—be indifferent to them!"

"Ultimately, this is specifically how you will benefit—it's worth it!"

In modern communication, this is the approach that is suggested: get to the point first and then start expanding. Well, Patanjali had already realised this! If you delay speaking of the goal, you will lose the reader's interest! Clever!

The second communication technique you will see is the structured outside-in method. Two examples exemplify this.

One: The elaboration of the movement from the yamas through the niyamas through the asanas through pranayama through pratyahara through dharana through dhyana and finally samadhi. Bahiranga to antaranga. This structured method appeals to our longing for order and method and makes us appreciate the eight limbs better.

Two: This is also true when he describes the four steps of samprajnata—starting with focusing on an external object and then moving inwards. This "hand-holding" gives confidence to the yogi.

It is never what you say but how you say it!

Patanjali clearly understood that if he wrote about the restless mind, he ought to get to the point quickly, or the restless reader's attention would wander away! In these days of mobile phones, where people are so easily distracted and move from one screen of information to another, Patanjali's methods continue to be relevant and appropriate.

This principle of tight communication is seen through all the 196 sutras! Each line is a masterpiece. Each line lends itself to immense study. He starts by saying, "Now starts the disciple on yoga." He ends with, "And that is it!"

Much has been written by others more qualified than me about our great spiritual heritage. The concepts of karma and dharma, the Vedas, the Upanishads and so on. Each topic is a bottomless ocean and leaves the student in awe of the intellect of the persons who were able to articulate such ideas.

The Yoga Sutras, likewise, represent, in my opinion, a tight and brilliant philosophy that explains—well, everything! Kleshas, gunas, karma, viveka, samskaras, the limbs of yoga, purusha, samyama, kaivalya and many more—such beautiful concepts, each capable of drawing tears of respect from the eyes of the reader. The whole idea that there is a collective consciousness that we are a part of and which we shall merge with is sophisticated.

Patanjali demonstrates a deep understanding of human psychology—why do we do what we do, why do we repeat self-destructive acts, why do we constantly fail to appreciate the real "I" and identify our engagement with the external world as representing "I" and so on. There is a larger purpose for all this, and he says so beautifully—"The seen exists for the seer." He is hoping that the reader realises that the gunas are playing with us.

Is there any moralising or lecturing by Patanjali? At first sight, the description of the yamas and niyamas—of ahimsa, truthfulness, not stealing and so on—suggests that. But the intent is different.

Once you realise what yoga is truly about, you need to condition your mind. It must first be made pure, soft and receptive for the journey ahead. In fact, even before the description of the eight limbs of yoga, Patanjali advises us to look at the components of kriya yoga. The intent is this: quieten your mind and make it mellow, let good intent flood it, bring in peace, goodwill and faith.

Patanjali, the psychologist, knows what works!

Powers

The three limbs—dharana, dhyana and samadhi—are strategically placed at the beginning of the Vibhuti Pada. It is the stage of the journey within, and the idea of samyama is expressed. Once you get it, Patanjali explains what happens when the yogi practises samyama.

The concepts of dharma, lakshana, avastha (let's call them DLA!) gives us an important insight into a great fundamental "oneness". An exalted yogi who "gets DLA" releases the floodgates of powerful abilities through applying samyama on various objects, tangible and intangible.

But this is not about demonstrating power—it is only to acknowledge what could happen to the yogi when he practises samyama. The specific abilities, like transmigration, changes in size and weight, the ability to levitate and understand all languages, etc.—are interesting in their own right. But—and this is a very important but—these powers are to be ignored and only used in unusual situations and certainly not for one's own benefit. In a sense, these derivative powers are allurements to the yogi and there is every possibility he would succumb. Which he must guard against, of course, because there are many more important things at stake.

In general, bringing this back to our routine lives, we see a humbling principle in action: whatever refined skill you acquire, whatever wealth you accumulate, whatever extra you happen to possess—do not be enamoured by them. Keep a distance. It is not *you*. It is something you possess, which you can lose in an instant. Possession of power implies great responsibility and judgement. Exercise that power with care.

In the Kaivalya Pada, Patanjali invokes this principle in the most beautiful way, describing the letting go of all acquired knowledge as the yogi slips into dharma-megha samadhi, where he is showered by virtue and is radiantly alone.

And so much more in those 196 lines.

As I read, I understood why Patanjali's Yoga Sutras is considered one of the foundational texts of Indian culture. It is a literary, philosophical and spiritual heritage to be very respectful and proud of. Very few texts have plumbed such depths to explain such challenging ideas.

In my interpretation, I have often referred to certain cultural sensibilities that have flowed into our thinking over generations. It is a great gift. We instinctively and respectfully appreciate the ideas of karma, rebirth and so on. Words used in our languages, conversational injections ("It is his karma!" or "He seems to be an evolved soul!"), birth and death rituals ("Let us pray he attains moksha") and daily routines—all contain allusions to these great philosophical thoughts that have descended through the ages and diffused throughout the geography of ancient India.

We live comfortably in paradoxes today, oftentimes deeply entrenched in the frenzy of the world while still maintaining hooks into our heritage, which we can fall back on from time to time. Relish it! This gift is not available to many in other countries. There is no serious historical or cultural safety net of similar philosophical thought to clutch save the sophisticated thoughts of Jung and some others in relatively modern times.

As I understood and interpreted the of Patanjali, I concluded that they represent the literary apex of rarefied, comprehensive knowledge expressed tightly, cogently and logically. Merely reading them is a privilege as they give a whiff of the powerful radiant energy of a brilliant intellect, with powers of discernment and insight like none other.

Moments of sharp understanding. Flashes of acute comprehension. Mysteries resolved in single lines. Everything explained.

Patanjali's Yoga Sutras. A map for he who seeks the meaning of life.

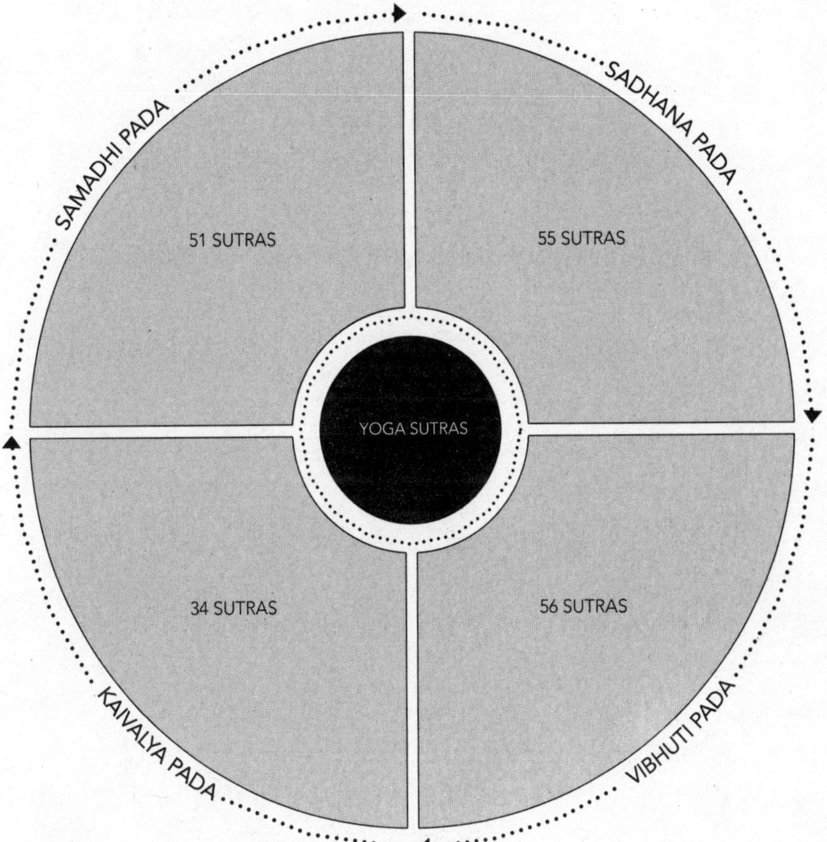
SAMADHI PADA
SADHANA PADA
VIBHUTI PADA
KAIVALYA PADA
51 SUTRAS
55 SUTRAS
34 SUTRAS
56 SUTRAS
YOGA SUTRAS

Acknowledgements

Sometime in 2021, I received an unexpected call from Akash Shah, the publisher of Jaico Publishing House. I was minding my own business, leading a placid life, and was not in a writing mood at all. Writing about yoga was the last thing on my mind.

Akash gently persuaded me to write this book, knowing that I was a yoga enthusiast. I didn't need much of a push and began immediately. I am grateful to him for his vote of confidence.

Writing is a solitary pursuit. It might appear glamorous. It is not. There are periods of self-doubt and of low productivity. Sometimes you are "not in the mood", and sometimes you write thousands of words in an inspired rush. But when all the dust settles, it is a competent editor who needs to help bring the work to life. In this endeavour, Jaico's editorial team proved to be a group of editorial perfectionists who gave me the precise inputs needed to transform my efforts into something solid.

In all efforts, it is wise to bow your head in the presence of someone who is an authority on the subject. The Yoga Sutras has captured the attention of mystics and philosophers for centuries. Deciphering the text and resolving contradictions was very challenging, and I often despaired that I was not "getting it".

I was very fortunate to have been introduced to Dr. Ananda Balayogi Bhavanani of the Centre for Yoga Therapy, Education and Research, Pondicherry, by a common friend, Dr. Manjiri Prabhu, herself a renowned writer. At various points during the writing of this book, I consulted him by phone or email and sought his guidance. He was generous with his advice and encouraged me with great warmth. I consider myself very lucky. Thank you, sir.

Smriti Sundar, a young yoga enthusiast and an artist, took up the challenge of creating illustrations that were so necessary to augment certain concepts. I am sure you will like her elegant work. Thank you, Smriti!

Of course, friends and family supported me throughout by reading early drafts and pointing out errors or places where I could have expressed myself better. I thank them all.

It might seem dramatic to say this, but I believe there was someone invisible who held my hand and helped me articulate my understanding. I am referring to Sage Patanjali, who elevated my own thinking during the process of reading his masterpiece. Each sutra was laden with brilliance and multiple layers of piercing insights. He gave me the strength to write this. All mistakes and misinterpretations are mine. All credit to him, who crafted one of the greatest contributions of our civilisation, the philosophy of yoga, which we now offer freely to the world.

Vasudev Murthy
Bangalore

Appendix

The Yoga Sutras in Devanagari with its English transliteration

पातञ्जलयोगसूत्राणि

Patanjali Yogasutrani

॥ महर्षि पतञ्जलि प्रणीतं योगदर्शनम् ॥

Maharishi Patanjali Pranitam Yogadarshanam

॥ प्रथमोऽध्याय: ॥ ॥ समाधि-पाद: ॥ (SAMADHI PADA)

Samadhi Padah

Chapter 1

1	अथ योगानुशासनम् ॥ १.१ ॥
	atha yoga-anuśāsanam
2	योगश्चित्तवृत्तिनिरोध: ॥ १.२ ॥
	yogaś-citta-vrtti-nirodhaḥ
3	तदा द्रष्टु: स्वरूपेऽवस्थानम् ॥ १.३ ॥
	tadā draṣṭuḥ svarūpe- 'vasthānam
4	वृत्तिसारूप्यमितरत्र ॥ १.४ ॥
	vrtti sārūpyam-itaratra

5	वृत्तयः पञ्चतय्यः क्लिष्टाऽक्लिष्टाः ॥ १.५ ॥
	vrttayaḥ pañcatayyaḥ kliṣṭākliṣṭāḥ
6	प्रमाणविपर्ययविकल्पनिद्रास्मृतयः ॥ १.६ ॥
	pramāṇa viparyaya vikalpa nidrā smrtayaḥ
7	प्रत्यक्षानुमानागमाः प्रमाणानि ॥ १.७ ॥
	pratyakṣa-anumāna-āgamāḥ pramāṇāni
8	विपर्ययो मिथ्याज्ञानमतद्रूपप्रतिष्ठम् ॥ १.८ ॥
	viparyayo mithyā-jñānam-atadrūpa pratiṣṭham
9	शब्दज्ञानानुपाती वस्तुशून्यो विकल्पः ॥ १.९ ॥
	śabda-jñāna-anupātī vastu-śūnyo vikalpaḥ
10	अभावप्रत्ययालम्बना वृत्तिर्निद्रा ॥ १.१० ॥
	abhāva pratyayālambanā vrttirnidrā
11	अनुभूतविषयासंप्रमोषः स्मृतिः ॥ १.११ ॥
	anu-bhūta-viṣaya-asaṁpramoṣaḥ smrtiḥ
12	अभ्यासवैराग्याभ्यां तन्निरोधः ॥ १.१२ ॥
	abhyāsa vairāgyābhyām tannirōdhaḥ
13	तत्र स्थितौ यत्नोऽभ्यासः ॥ १.१३ ॥
	tatra sthitau yatno- 'bhyāsaḥ
14	स तु दीर्घकालनैरन्तर्यसत्कारासेवितो दृढभूमिः ॥ १.१४ ॥
	sa tu dīrghakāla nairantarya satkāra-āsevito drḍhabhūmiḥ
15	दृष्टानुश्रविकविषयवितृष्णस्य वशीकारसंज्ञा वैराग्यम् ॥ १.१५ ॥
	drṣṭa-anuśravika-viṣaya-vitrṣṇasya vaśīkāra-saṁjṇā vairāgyam
16	तत्परं पुरुषख्यातेर्गुणवैतृष्ण्यम् ॥ १.१६ ॥
	tatparaṁ puruṣa-khyāteḥ guṇa-vaitrṣṇyam
17	वितर्कविचारानन्दास्मितारूपानुगमात् संप्रज्ञातः ॥ १.१७ ॥
	vitarka-vicāra-ānanda-asmitā-rūpa-anugamāt-saṁprajñātaḥ
18	विरामप्रत्ययाभ्यासपूर्वः संस्कारशेषोऽन्यः ॥ १.१८ ॥
	virāma-pratyaya-abhyāsa-pūrvaḥ saṁskāra-śeṣo- 'nyaḥ
19	भवप्रत्ययो विदेहप्रकृतिलयानाम् ॥ १.१९ ॥
	bhava-pratyayo videha-prakrti-layānām
20	श्रद्धावीर्यस्मृतिसमाधिप्रज्ञापूर्वक इतरेषाम् ॥ १.२० ॥
	śraddhā-vīrya-smrti samādhi-prajñā-pūrvaka itareṣām

21	तीव्रसंवेगानामासन्नः ॥ १.२१ ॥
	tīvra-saṁvegānām-āsannaḥ
22	मृदुमध्याधिमात्रत्वात् ततोऽपि विशेषः ॥ १.२२ ॥
	mrdu-madhya-adhimātratvāt-tato'pi viśeṣaḥ
23	ईश्वरप्रणिधानाद्वा ॥ १.२३ ॥
	īśvara-praṇidhānād-vā
24	क्लेशकर्मविपाकाशयैरपरामृष्टः पुरुषविशेष ईश्वरः ॥ १.२४ ॥
	kleśa karma vipāka-āśayaiḥ-aparāmrṣṭaḥ puruṣa-viśeṣa īśvaraḥ
25	तत्र निरतिशयं सार्वज्ञबीजम् ॥ १.२५ ॥
	tatra niratiśayaṁ sarvajña-bījam
26	स पूर्वेषामपि गुरुः कालेनानवच्छेदात् ॥ १.२६ ॥
	sa eṣa pūrveṣām-api-guruḥ kālena-anavacchedāt
27	तस्य वाचकः प्रणवः ॥ १.२७ ॥
	tasya vācakaḥ praṇavaḥ
28	तज्जपस्तदर्थभावनम् ॥ १.२८ ॥
	taj-japaḥ tad-artha-bhāvanam

Chapter 2

29	ततः प्रत्यक्चेतनाधिगमोऽप्यन्तरायाभावश्च ॥ १.२९ ॥
	tataḥ pratyak-cetana-adhigamo- 'py-antarāya-abhavaś-ca
30	व्याधिस्त्यानसंशयप्रमादालस्याविरति-भ्रान्तिदर्शनालब्धभूमिकत्वानवस्थितत्वानि चित्तविक्षेपास्तेऽन्तरायाः ॥ १.३० ॥
	vyādhi styāna saṁśaya pramāda-ālasya-avirati bhrāntidarśana-alabdha-bhūmikatva-anavasthitatvāni cittavikṣepāste'ntarāyāḥ
31	दुःखदौर्मनस्याङ्गमेजयत्वश्वासप्रश्वासा विक्षेपसहभुवः ॥ १.३१ ॥
	duḥkha-daurmanasya-aṅgamejayatva-śvāsapraśvāsāḥ vikṣepa sahabhuvaḥ
32	तत्प्रतिषेधार्थमेकतत्त्वाभ्यासः ॥ १.३२ ॥
	tat-pratiṣedha-artham-eka-tattva-abhyāsaḥ
33	मैत्रीकरुणामुदितोपेक्षाणां सुखदुःखपुण्यापुण्यविषयाणां भावनातश्चित्तप्रसादनम् ॥ १.३३ ॥
	maitrī karuṇā mudito-pekṣāṇāṁ-sukha-duḥkha puṇya-apuṇya-viṣayāṇāṁ bhāvanātaḥ citta-prasadanam
34	प्रच्छर्दनविधारणाभ्यां वा प्राणस्य ॥ १.३४ ॥
	pracchardana-vidhāraṇa-ābhyāṁ vā prāṇasya

35	विषयवती वा प्रवृत्तिरुत्पन्ना मनसः स्थितिनिबन्धिनी ॥ १.३५ ॥
	viṣayavatī vā pravrtti-rutpannā manasaḥ sthiti nibandhinī
36	विशोका वा ज्योतिष्मती ॥ १.३६ ॥
	viśokā vā jyotiṣmatī
37	वीतरागविषयं वा चित्तम् ॥ १.३७ ॥
	vītarāga viṣayam vā cittam
38	स्वप्ननिद्राज्ञानालम्बनं वा ॥ १.३८ ॥
	svapna-nidrā jñāna-ālambanam vā
39	यथाभिमतध्यानाद्वा ॥ १.३९ ॥
	yathā-abhimata-dhyānād-vā
40	परमाणु परममहत्त्वान्तोऽस्य वशीकारः ॥ १.४० ॥
	paramāṇu parama-mahattva-anto- 'sya vaśīkāraḥ
41	क्षीणवृत्तेरभिजातस्येव मणेर्ग्रहीतृग्रहणग्राह्येषु तत्स्थतदञ्जनता समापत्तिः ॥ १.४१ ॥
	kṣīṇa-vrtter-abhijātasy-eva maṇer-grahītr-grahaṇa-grāhyeṣu tatstha-tadañjanatā samāpattiḥ
42	तत्र शब्दार्थज्ञानविकल्पैः संकीर्णा सवितर्का समापत्तिः ॥ १.४२ ॥
	tatra śabdārtha-jñāna-vikalpaiḥ saṁkīrṇā savitarkā samāpattiḥ
43	स्मृतिपरिशुद्धौ स्वरूपशून्येवार्थमात्रनिर्भासा निर्वितर्का ॥ १.४३ ॥
	smrti-pariśuddhau svarūpa-śūnyeva-arthamātra-nirbhāsā nirvitarkā
44	एतयैव सविचारा निर्विचारा च सूक्ष्मविषया व्याख्याता ॥ १.४४ ॥
	etayaiva savicārā nirvicārā ca sūkṣma-viṣaya vyākhyātā
45	सूक्ष्मविषयत्वं चालिङ्गपर्यवसानम् ॥ १.४५ ॥
	sūkṣma-viṣayatvam-ca-aliṅga paryavasānam
46	ता एव सबीजः समाधिः ॥ १.४६ ॥
	tā eva sabījas-samādhiḥ
47	निर्विचारवैशारद्येऽध्यात्मप्रसादः ॥ १.४७ ॥
	nirvicāra-vaiśāradye- 'dhyātma-prasādaḥ
48	ऋतम्भरा तत्र प्रज्ञा ॥ १.४८ ॥
	rtaṁbharā tatra prajñā
49	श्रुतानुमानप्रज्ञाभ्यामन्यविषया विशेषार्थत्वात् ॥ १.४९ ॥
	śruta-anumāna-prajñā-abhyām-anya-viṣayā viśeṣa-arthatvāt
50	तज्जः संस्कारोऽन्यसंस्कारप्रतिबन्धी ॥ १.५० ॥
	tajjas-saṁskāro- 'nya-saṁskāra pratibandhī

51	तस्यापि निरोधे सर्वनिरोधान्निर्बीजः समाधिः ॥ १.५१ ॥
	tasyāpi nirodhe sarva-nirodhān-nirbījaḥ samādhiḥ
	॥ इति पतञ्जलि-विरचिते योग-सूत्रे प्रथमः समाधि-पादः ॥
	Iti Patanjali virchite yoga sutre prathamah samadhi padah

॥ द्वितीयोऽध्यायः ॥ ॥ साधन-पादः ॥ (SADHAṆA PADA)

Dwitiyo Adhyayah Sadhana Padah

Chapter 3

1	तपःस्वाध्यायेश्वरप्रणिधानानि क्रियायोगः ॥ २.१ ॥
	tapaḥ svādhyāy-eśvarapraṇidhānāni kriyā-yogaḥ
2	समाधिभावनार्थः क्लेशतनूकरणार्थश्च ॥ २.२ ॥
	samādhi-bhāvana-arthaḥ kleśa tanū-karaṇa-arthaś-ca
3	अविद्यास्मितारागद्वेषाभिनिवेशाः क्लेशाः ॥ २.३ ॥
	avidyā-asmitā-rāga-dveṣa-abhiniveśaḥ kleśāḥ
4	अविद्या क्षेत्रमुत्तरेषां प्रसुप्ततनुविच्छिन्नोदाराणाम् ॥ २.४ ॥
	avidyā kṣetram-uttareṣām prasupta-tanu-vicchinn-odārāṇām
5	अनित्याशुचिदुःखानात्मसु नित्यशुचिसुखात्मख्यातिरविद्या ॥ २.५ ॥
	anityā-aśuci-duḥkha-anātmasu nitya-śuci-sukha-ātmakhyātir-avidyā
6	दृग्दर्शनशक्त्योरेकात्मतेवास्मिता ॥ २.६ ॥
	drg-darśana-śaktyor-ekātmata-iva-asmitā
7	सुखानुशयी रागः ॥ २.७ ॥
	sukha-anuśayī rāgaḥ
8	दुःखानुशयी द्वेषः ॥ २.८ ॥
	duḥkha-anuśayī dveṣaḥ
9	स्वरसवाही विदुषोऽपि तथारूढोऽभिनिवेशः ॥ २.९ ॥
	svarasvāhi viduṣo- 'pi samārūḍho- 'bhiniveśaḥ
10	ते प्रतिप्रसवहेयाः सूक्ष्माः ॥ २.१० ॥
	te pratiprasava-heyāḥ sūkṣmāḥ
11	ध्यानहेयास्तद्वृत्तयः ॥ २.११ ॥
	dhyāna heyāḥ tad-vrttayaḥ

12	क्लेशमूलः कर्माशयो दृष्टादृष्टजन्मवेदनीयः ॥ २.१२ ॥
	kleśa-mūlaḥ karma-aśayo drṣṭa-adrṣṭa-janma-vedanīyaḥ
13	सति मूले तद्विपाको जात्यायुर्भोगाः ॥ २.१३ ॥
	sati mūle tad-vipāko jāty-āyur-bhogāḥ
14	ते ह्लादपरितापफलाः पुण्यापुण्यहेतुत्वात् ॥ २.१४ ॥
	te hlāda paritāpa-phalāḥ puṇya-apuṇya-hetutvāt
15	परिणामतापसंस्कारदुःखैर्गुणवृत्तिविरोधाच्च दुःखमेव सर्वं विवेकिनः ॥ २.१५ ॥
	pariṇāma tāpa saṁskāra duḥkhaiḥ guṇa-vrtti-virodhācca duḥkham-eva sarvaṁ vivekinaḥ
16	हेयं दुःखमनागतम् ॥ २.१६ ॥
	heyaṁ duḥkham-anāgatam
17	द्रष्टृदृश्ययोः संयोगो हेयहेतुः ॥ २.१७ ॥
	draṣṭr-drśyayoḥ saṁyogo heyahetuḥ
18	प्रकाशक्रियास्थितिशीलं भूतेन्द्रियात्मकं भोगापवर्गार्थं दृश्यम् ॥ २.१८ ॥
	prakāśa-kriyā-sthiti-śīlaṁ bhūtendriya-ātmakaṁ bhoga-apavarga-arthaṁ drśyam
19	विशेषाविशेषलिङ्गमात्रालिङ्गानि गुणपर्वाणि ॥ २.१९ ॥
	viśeṣa-aviśeṣa-liṅga-mātra-aliṅgāni guṇaparvāṇi
20	द्रष्टा दृशिमात्रः शुद्धोऽपि प्रत्ययानुपश्यः ॥ २.२० ॥
	draṣṭā drśimātraḥ śuddho-'pi pratyaya-anupaśyaḥ
21	तदर्थ एव दृश्यस्यात्मा ॥ २.२१ ॥
	tadartha eva drśyasya-ātmā
22	कृतार्थं प्रति नष्टमप्यनष्टं तदन्यसाधारणत्वात् ॥ २.२२ ॥
	krtārthaṁ pratinaṣṭaṁ-apy-anaṣṭaṁ tadanya sādhāraṇatvāt
23	स्वस्वामिशक्त्योः स्वरूपोपलब्धिहेतुः संयोगः ॥ २.२३ ॥
	svasvāmi-śaktyoḥ svarūp-oplabdhi-hetuḥ saṁyogaḥ
24	तस्य हेतुरविद्या ॥ २.२४ ॥
	tasya hetur-avidyā
25	तदभावात् संयोगाभावो हानं तद्दृशेः कैवल्यम् ॥ २.२५ ॥
	tad-abhābāt-saṁyoga-abhāvo hānaṁ taddrśeḥ kaivalyam
26	विवेकख्यातिरविप्लवा हानोपायः ॥ २.२६ ॥
	viveka-khyātir-aviplavā hānopāyaḥ
27	तस्य सप्तधा प्रान्तभूमिः प्रज्ञा ॥ २.२७ ॥
	asya saptadhā prānta-bhūmiḥ prajña

28	योगाङ्गानुष्ठानादशुद्धिक्षये ज्ञानदीप्तिरा विवेकख्यातेः ॥ २.२८ ॥
	yoga-aṅga-anuṣṭhānād-aśuddhi-kṣaye jñāna-dīptir-āviveka-khyāteḥ

Chapter 4

29	यमनियमासनप्राणायामप्रत्याहारधारणाध्यानसमाधयोऽष्टावङ्गानि ॥ २.२९ ॥
	yama niyama-āsana prāṇāyāma pratyāhāra dhāraṇā dhyāna samādhayo- 'ṣṭāvaṅgāni
30	अहिंसासत्यास्तेयब्रह्मचर्यापरिग्रहा यमाः ॥ २.३० ॥
	ahiṁsā-satya-asteya brahmacarya-aparigrahāḥ yamāḥ
31	जातिदेशकालसमयानवच्छिन्नाः सार्वभौमा महाव्रतम् ॥ २.३१ ॥
	jāti-deśa-kāla-samaya-anavacchinnāḥ sārvabhaumā-mahāvratam
32	शौचसंतोषतपःस्वाध्यायेश्वरप्रणिधानानि नियमाः ॥ २.३२ ॥
	śauca saṁtoṣa tapaḥ svādhyāy-eśvarapraṇidhānāni niyamāḥ
33	वितर्कबाधने प्रतिपक्षभावनम् ॥ २.३३ ॥
	vitarka-bādhane pratiprakṣa-bhāvanam
34	वितर्का हिंसादयः कृतकारितानुमोदिता लोभक्रोधमोहपूर्वका मृदुमध्याधिमात्रा दुःखाज्ञानानन्तफला इति प्रतिपक्षभावनम् ॥ २.३४ ॥
	vitarkā hiṁsādayaḥ krta-kārita-anumoditā lobha-krodha-moha-āpūrvakā mrdu-madhya adhi
35	अहिंसाप्रतिष्ठायां तत्सन्निधौ वैरत्यागः ॥ २.३५ ॥
	ahiṁsā-pratiṣṭhāyaṁ tat-sannidhau vairatyāghaḥ
36	सत्यप्रतिष्ठायां क्रियाफलाश्रयत्वम् ॥ २.३६ ॥
	satya-pratiṣthāyaṁ kriyā-phala-āśrayatvam
37	अस्तेयप्रतिष्ठायां सर्वरत्नोपस्थानम् ॥ २.३७ ॥
	asteya-pratiṣṭhāyāṁ sarvaratn-opasthānam
38	ब्रह्मचर्यप्रतिष्ठायां वीर्यलाभः ॥ २.३८ ॥
	brahma-carya pratiṣṭhāyāṁ vīrya-lābhaḥ
39	अपरिग्रहस्थैर्ये जन्मकथंतासम्बोधः ॥ २.३९ ॥
	aparigraha-sthairye janma-kathaṁtā saṁbodhaḥ
40	शौचात् स्वाङ्गजुगुप्सा परैरसंसर्गः ॥ २.४० ॥
	śaucāt svāṅga-jugupsā parairasaṁsargaḥ
41	सत्त्वशुद्धिसौमनस्यैकाग्र्येन्द्रियजयात्मदर्शन-योग्यत्वानि च ॥ २.४१ ॥
	sattva-śuddhiḥ saumanasya-ikāgry-endriyajaya-ātmadarśana yogyatvāni ca

42	संतोषादनुत्तमसुखलाभः ॥ २.४२ ॥
	saṁtoṣāt-anuttamas-sukhalābhaḥ
43	कायेन्द्रियसिद्धिरशुद्धिक्षयात् तपसः ॥ २.४३ ॥
	kāyendriya-siddhir-aśuddhi-kṣayāt tapasaḥ
44	स्वाध्यायाद् इष्टदेवतासंप्रयोगः ॥ २.४४ ॥
	svādhyāyād-iṣṭa-devatā saṁprayogaḥ
45	समाधिसिद्धिरीश्वरप्रणिधानात् ॥ २.४५ ॥
	samādhi siddhiḥ-īśvarapraṇidhānāt
46	स्थिरसुखम् आसनम् ॥ २.४६ ॥
	sthira-sukham-āsanam
47	प्रयत्नशैथिल्यानन्तसमापत्तिभ्याम् ॥ २.४७ ॥
	prayatna-śaithilya-ananta-samāpatti-bhyām
48	ततो द्वन्द्वानभिघातः ॥ २.४८ ॥
	tato dvaṅdva-an-abhighātaḥ
49	तस्मिन्सति श्वासप्रश्वासयोर्गतिविच्छेदः प्राणायामः ॥ २.४९ ॥
	tasmin sati śvāsa-praśvāsyor-gati-vicchedaḥ prāṇāyāmaḥ
50	बाह्याभ्यन्तरस्तम्भवृत्तिर्देशकालसंख्याभिः परिदृष्टो दीर्घसूक्ष्मः ॥ २.५० ॥
	bāhya-ābhyantara-sthambha vrttiḥ deśa-kāla-sankhyābhiḥ paridrṣṭo dīrgha-sūkṣmaḥ
51	बाह्याभ्यन्तरविषयाक्षेपी चतुर्थः ॥ २.५१ ॥
	bāhya-ābhyantara viṣaya-akṣepī caturthaḥ
52	ततः क्षीयते प्रकाशावरणम् ॥ २.५२ ॥
	tataḥ kṣīyate prakāśa-āvaraṇam
53	धारणासु च योग्यता मनसः ॥ २.५३ ॥
	dhāraṇāsu ca yogyatā manasaḥ
54	स्वविषयासंप्रयोगे चित्तस्वरूपानुकार इवेन्द्रियाणां प्रत्याहारः ॥ २.५४ ॥
	svaviṣaya-asaṁprayoge cittasya svarūpānukāra-iv-endriyāṇāṁ pratyāhāraḥ
55	ततः परमा वश्यतेन्द्रियाणाम् ॥ २.५५ ॥
	tataḥ paramā-vaśyatā indriyāṇām
	॥ इति पतञ्जलि-विरचिते योग-सूत्रे द्वितीयः साधन-पादः ॥
	Iti Patanjali virchit yoga sutre Dwitiyah Sadhana Pada

॥ तृतीयोऽध्यायः ॥ ॥ विभूति-पादः ॥ (VIBHUTI PADA)

Tritaya Adhyayh Vibhuti Padah

Chapter 5

1	देशबन्धश्चित्तस्य धारणा ॥ ३.१ ॥
	deśa-bandhaḥ cittasya dhāraṇ
2	तत्र प्रत्ययैकतानता ध्यानम् ॥ ३.२ ॥
	tatra pratyaya-ikatānatā dhyānam
3	तदेवार्थमात्रनिर्भासं स्वरूपशून्यमिव समाधिः ॥ ३.३ ॥
	tadeva-artha-mātra-nirbhāsaṁ svarūpa-śūnyam-iva-samādhiḥ
4	त्रयमेकत्र संयमः ॥ ३.४ ॥
	trayam-ekatra saṁyamaḥ
5	तज्जयात्प्रज्ञालोकः ॥ ३.५ ॥
	tajjayāt prajñālokaḥ
6	तस्य भूमिषु विनियोगः ॥ ३.६ ॥
	tasya bhūmiṣu viniyogaḥ
7	त्रयमन्तरङ्गं पूर्वेभ्यः ॥ ३.७ ॥
	trayam-antarangaṁ pūrvebhyaḥ
8	तदपि बहिरङ्गं निर्बीजस्य ॥ ३.८ ॥
	tadapi bahiraṅgaṁ nirbījasy
9	व्युत्थाननिरोधसंस्कारयोरभिभवप्रादुर्भावौ निरोधक्षणचित्तान्वयो निरोधपरिणामः ॥ ३.९ ॥
	vyutthāna-nirodha-saṁskārayoḥ abhibhava-prādurbhāvau nirodhakṣaṇa cittānvayo nirodha-parinamah
10	तस्य प्रशान्तवाहिता संस्कारात् ॥ ३.१० ॥
	tasya praśānta-vāhitā saṁskārat
11	सर्वार्थतैकाग्रतयोः क्षयोदयौ चित्तस्य समाधिपरिणामः ॥ ३.११ ॥
	sarvārthatā ekāgrātayoḥ kṣayodayau cittasya samādhi-pariṇāmah
12	ततः पुनः शान्तोदितौ तुल्यप्रत्ययौ चित्तस्यैकाग्रतापरिणामः ॥ ३.१२ ॥
	tataḥ punaḥ śātoditau tulya-pratyayau cittasya-ikāgratā-pariṇāmaḥ
13	एतेन भूतेन्द्रियेषु धर्मलक्षणावस्थापरिणामा व्याख्याताः ॥ ३.१३ ॥
	etena bhūtendriyeṣu dharma-lakṣaṇa-avasthā pariṇāmā vyākhyātāḥ

14	शान्तोदिताव्यपदेश्यधर्मानुपाती धर्मी ॥ ३.१४ ॥
	śān-odita-avyapadeśya-dharmānupātī dharmī
15	क्रमान्यत्वं परिणामान्यत्वे हेतुः ॥ ३.१५ ॥
	kramānyatvaṁ pariṇāmānyateve hetuḥ
16	परिणामत्रयसंयमाद् अतीतानागतज्ञानम् ॥ ३.१६ ॥
	pariṇāmatraya-saṁyamāt-atītānāgata jñānam
17	शब्दार्थप्रत्ययानामितरेतराध्यासात् सङ्करस्तत्प्रविभागसंयमात्सर्वभूतरुतज्ञानम् ॥ ३.१७ ॥
	śabdartha-pratyayāmām-itaretarādhyāsāt-saṁkaraḥ tat-pravibhāga-saṁyamāt sarvabhūta-ruta- jñānam
18	संस्कारसाक्षात्करणात्पूर्वजातिज्ञानम् ॥ ३.१८ ॥
	saṁskāra-sākṣātkaraṇāt pūrva-jāti-jñānam
19	प्रत्ययस्य परचित्तज्ञानम् ॥ ३.१९ ॥
	pratyayasya para-citta-jñānam
20	न च तत्सालम्बनं तस्याविषयीभूतत्वात् ॥ ३.२० ॥
	na ca tat sālambanaṁ tasya-aviṣayī bhūtatvāt
21	कायरूपसंयमात्तद्ग्राह्यशक्तिस्तम्भे चक्षुःप्रकाशासंप्रयोगेऽन्तर्धानम् ॥ ३.२१ ॥
	kāya-rūpa-saṁyamāt tat-grāhyaśakti-stambhe cakṣuḥ prakāśāsaṁprayoge- 'ntardhānam
22	एतेन सब्ददी अन्तर्द्कनम उक्तम
	Etena sabdadi antardkanam uktam
23	सोपक्रमं निरुपक्रमं च कर्म तत्संयमादपरान्तज्ञानमरिष्टेभ्यो वा ॥ ३.२२ ॥
	sopa-kramaṁ nirupa-kramaṁ ca karma tatsaṁyamāt-aparāntajñānam ariṣṭebhyo vā
24	मैत्र्यादिषु बलानि ॥ ३.२३ ॥
	maitry-adiṣu balāni
25	बलेषु हस्तिबलादीनि ॥ ३.२४ ॥
	baleṣu hastibalādīnī
26	प्रवृत्त्यालोकन्यासात्सूक्ष्मव्यवहितविप्रकृष्टज्ञानम् ॥ ३.२५ ॥
	pravrtty-āloka-nyāsāt sūkṣmā-vyāvahita-viprakrṣṭa-jñānam
27	भुवनज्ञानं सूर्ये संयमात् ॥ ३.२६ ॥
	bhuva-jñānaṁ sūrye-saṁyamāt
28	चन्द्रे ताराव्यूहज्ञानम् ॥ ३.२७ ॥
	candre tāravyūha-jñānam

29	ध्रुवे तद्गतिज्ञानम् ॥ ३.२८ ॥ dhruve tadgati-jñānam
30	नाभिचक्रे कायव्यूहज्ञानम् ॥ ३.२९ ॥ nābhicakre kāyavyūha-jñānam
31	कण्ठकूपे क्षुत्पिपासानिवृत्तिः ॥ ३.३० ॥ kanṭha-kūpe kṣutpipāsā nivrttiḥ
32	कूर्मनाड्यां स्थैर्यम् ॥ ३.३१ ॥ kūrma-nāḍyāṁ sthairyam
33	मूर्धज्योतिषि सिद्धदर्शनम् ॥ ३.३२ ॥ mūrdha-jyotiṣi siddha-darśanam
34	प्रातिभाद्वा सर्वम् ॥ ३.३३ ॥ prātibhād-vā sarvam
35	हृदये चित्तसंवित् ॥ ३.३४ ॥ hrḍaye citta-saṁvit

Chapter 6

36	सत्त्वपुरुषयोरत्यन्तासंकीर्णयोः प्रत्ययाविशेषो भोगः परार्थत्वात्स्वार्थसंयमात्पुरुषज्ञानम् ॥ ३.३५ ॥ sattva-puruṣāyoḥ atyantā-saṁkīrṇayoḥ pratyayāviśeṣo-bhogaḥ para-arthat-vāt-sva-arthasaṁ
37	ततः प्रातिभश्रावणवेदनादर्शास्वादवार्ता जायन्ते ॥ ३.३६ ॥ tataḥ prātibha-srāvāṇa-vedana-ādarśa-āsvāda-vārtā jāyante
38	ते समाधावुपसर्गा व्युत्थाने सिद्धयः ॥ ३.३७ ॥ te samādhav-upasargā[ḥ]-vyutthāne siddhayaḥ
39	बन्धकारणशैथिल्यात्प्रचारसंवेदनाच्च चित्तस्य परशरीरावेशः ॥ ३.३८ ॥ badnha-kāraṇa-śaithilyāt pracāra-saṁvedanācca cittasya paraśarīrāveśaḥ
40	उदानजयाज्जलपङ्ककण्टकादिष्वसङ्ग उत्क्रान्तिश्च ॥ ३.३९ ॥ udāna-jayāat jala-paṇkha-kaṇṭakādiṣv-asaṅgo- 'tkrāntiśca
41	समानजयाज्ज्वलनम् ॥ ३.४० ॥ samāna-jayāj-jvalanam
42	श्रोत्राकाशयोः सम्बन्धसंयमाद्दिव्यं श्रोत्रम् ॥ ३.४१ ॥ Srotrakāyākāśayoḥ saṁbandha-saṁyamāt laghu-tūla-samāpatteśca-ākāśa gamanam

43	कायाकाशयोः सम्बन्धसंयमाल्लघुतूल-समापत्तेश्चाकाशगमनम् ॥ ३.४२ ॥
	kāyākāśayoḥ sambandhasaṃyamāllaghutūla-samāpatteścākāśagamanam
44	बहिरकल्पिता वृत्तिर्महाविदेहा ततः प्रकाशावरणक्षयः ॥ ३.४३ ॥
	bahir-akalpitā vrttiḥ mahā-videhā tataḥ prakāśa-āvaraṇa-kṣayaḥ
45	स्थूलस्वरूपसूक्ष्मान्वयार्थवत्त्वसंयमाद्भूतजयः ॥ ३.४४ ॥
	sthūla-svarūpa-sūkṣma-anvaya-arthavattva-saṁyamāt bhūtajayaḥ
46	ततोऽणिमादिप्रादुर्भावः कायसम्पत्तद्धर्मानभिघातश्च ॥ ३.४५ ॥
	tato-aṇimādi-prādurbhāvaḥ kāyasaṁpat tad-dharānabhighātśca
47	रूपलावण्यबलवज्रसंहननत्वानि कायसम्पत् ॥ ३.४६ ॥
	rūpa-lāvaṇya-bala-vajra-saṁhananatvāni kāyasaṁpat
48	ग्रहणस्वरूपास्मितान्वयार्थवत्त्वसंयमादिन्द्रियजयः ॥ ३.४७ ॥
	grahaṇa-svarūpa-asmitā-avaya-arthavattva-saṁyamāt-indriya jayaḥ
49	ततो मनोजवित्वं विकरणभावः प्रधानजयश्च ॥ ३.४८ ॥
	tato mano-javitvaṁ vikaraṇa-bhāvaḥ pradhāna-jayaś-ca
50	सत्त्वपुरुषान्यताख्यातिमात्रस्य सर्वभावाधिष्ठातृत्वं सर्वज्ञातृत्वं च ॥ ३.४९ ॥
	sattva-puruṣa-anyatā-khyātimātrasya sarva-bhāvā-adhiṣṭhātrtvaṁ sarva-jñātrtvaṁ ca
51	तद्वैराग्यादपि दोषबीजक्षये कैवल्यम् ॥ ३.५० ॥
	tad-vairāgyād-api doṣa-bīja-kṣaye kaivalyam
52	स्थान्युपनिमन्त्रणे सङ्गस्मयाकरणं पुनरनिष्टप्रसङ्गात् ॥ ३.५१ ॥
	sthāny-upa-nimantraṇe saṅga-smaya-akaraṇaṁ punar-aniṣṭa-prasaṅgāt
53	क्षणतत्क्रमयोः संयमाद्विवेकजं ज्ञानम् ॥ ३.५२ ॥
	kṣaṇa-tat-kramayoḥ saṁyamāt vivekajaṁ-jñānam
54	जातिलक्षणदेशैरन्यतानवच्छेदात् तुल्ययोस्ततः प्रतिपत्तिः ॥ ३.५३ ॥
	jāti-lakṣaṇa-deśaiḥ anyatā-anavacchedāt tulyayoḥ tataḥ pratipattiḥ
55	तारकं सर्वविषयं सर्वथाविषयम् अक्रमं चेति विवेकजं ज्ञानम् ॥ ३.५४ ॥
	tārakaṁ sarva-viṣayaṁ sarvathā-viṣayam-akramaṁ-ceti vivekajaṁ jñānam
56	सत्त्वपुरुषयोः शुद्धिसाम्ये कैवल्यमिति ॥ ३.५५ ॥
	sattva-puruṣayoḥ śuddhisāmye kaivalyam

	॥ इति पतञ्जलि-विरचिते योग-सूत्रे तृतीयो विभूति-पादः ॥
	Iti Patanjali virchite Yoga sutre Tritiya Vibhuti Padah

॥ चतुर्थोऽध्यायः ॥ ॥ कैवल्य-पादः ॥ (KAIVALYA PADA)

Chaturadhyayh Kaivalya Padah

Chapter 7

1	जन्मौषधिमन्त्रतपःसमाधिजाः सिद्धयः ॥ ४.१ ॥
	janma-oṣadhi-mantra-tapas-samādhi-jāḥ siddhayaḥ
2	जात्यन्तरपरिणामः प्रकृत्यापूरात् ॥ ४.२ ॥
	jāty-antara-pariṇāmaḥ prakrty-āpūrāt
3	निमित्तमप्रयोजकं प्रकृतीनां वरणभेदस्तु ततः क्षेत्रिकवत् ॥ ४.३ ॥
	nimittam-aprayojakaṁ prakrtīnāṁ-varaṇa-bhedastu tataḥ kṣetrikavat
4	निर्माणचित्तान्यस्मितामात्रात् ॥ ४.४ ॥
	nirmāṇa-cittāny-asmitā-mātrāt
5	प्रवृत्तिभेदे प्रयोजकं चित्तमेकमनेकेषाम् ॥ ४.५ ॥
	pravrtti-bhede prayojakaṁ cittam-ekam-anekeṣām
6	तत्र ध्यानजमनाशयम् ॥ ४.६ ॥
	tatra dhyānajam-anāśayam
7	कर्माशुक्लाकृष्णं योगिनस्त्रिविधमितरेषाम् ॥ ४.७ ॥
	karma-aśukla-akrṣṇaṁ *yoginaḥ* trividham-itareṣām
8	ततस्तद्विपाकानुगुणानामेवाभिव्यक्तिर्वासनानाम् ॥ ४.८ ॥
	tataḥ tad-vipāka-anugṇānām-eva-abhivyaktiḥ vāsanānām
9	जातिदेशकालव्यवहितानामप्यानन्तर्यं स्मृतिसंस्कारयोरेकरूपत्वात् ॥ ४.९ ॥
	jāti deśa kāla vyavahitānām-apy-āntaryāṁ smrti-saṁskārayoḥ ekarūpatvāt
10	तासामनादित्वं चाशिषो नित्यत्वात् ॥ ४.१० ॥
	tāsām-anāditvaṁ cāśiṣo nityatvāt
11	हेतुफलाश्रयालम्बनैः संगृहीतत्वादेषामभावे तदभावः ॥ ४.११ ॥
	hetu-phala-āśraya-ālambanaiḥ-saṁgrhītatvāt-eṣām-abhāve-tad-abhāvaḥ
12	अतीतानागतं स्वरूपतोऽस्त्यध्वभेदाद्धर्माणाम् ॥ ४.१२ ॥
	atīta-anāgataṁ svarūpato- 'sti-adhvabhedād dharmāṇām

13	ते व्यक्तसूक्ष्मा गुणात्मानः ॥ ४.१३ ॥
	te vyakta-sūkṣmāḥ guṇa-atmānaḥ
14	परिणामैकत्वाद्वस्तुतत्त्वम् ॥ ४.१४ ॥
	pariṇāma-ikatvāt vastu-tattvam
15	वस्तुसाम्ये चित्तभेदात्तयोर्विभक्तः पन्थाः ॥ ४.१५ ॥
	vastusāmye citta-bhedāt-tayorvibhaktaḥ panthāḥ
16	न चैकचित्ततन्त्रं वस्तु तदप्रमाणकं तदा किं स्यात् ॥ ४.१६ ॥
	na caika-citta-tantraṁ vastu tad-apramāṇakaṁ tadā kiṁ syāt
17	तदुपरागापेक्षित्वाच्चित्तस्य वस्तु ज्ञाताज्ञातम् ॥ ४.१७ ॥
	tad-uparāga-apekṣitvāt cittasya vastu-jñātajñātaṁ

Chapter 8

18	सदा ज्ञाताश्चित्तवृत्तयस्तत्प्रभोः पुरुषस्यापरिणामित्वात् ॥ ४.१८ ॥
	sadājñātāḥ citta-vrttayaḥ tat-prabhoḥ puruṣasya-apariṇāmitvāt
19	न तत्स्वाभासं दृश्यत्वात् ॥ ४.१९ ॥
	na tat-svābhāsaṁ drśyatvāt
20	एकसमये चोभयानवधारणम् ॥ ४.२० ॥
	eka samaye c-obhaya-an-avadhāraṇam
21	चित्तान्तरदृश्ये बुद्धिबुद्धेरतिप्रसङ्गः स्मृतिसङ्करश्च ॥ ४.२१ ॥
	cittāntara drśye buddhi-buddheḥ atiprasaṅgaḥ smrti-saṁkaraś-ca
22	चितेरप्रतिसंक्रमायास्तदाकारापत्तौ स्वबुद्धिसंवेदनम् ॥ ४.२२ ॥
	citer-aprati-saṁkramāyāḥ tad-ākāra-āpattau svabuddhi saṁ-vedanam
23	द्रष्टृदृश्योपरक्तं चित्तं सर्वार्थम् ॥ ४.२३ ॥
	draṣṭr-drśy-opa-raktaṁ cittaṁ sarva-artham
24	तदसंख्येयवासनाभिश्चित्रमपि परार्थं संहत्यकारित्वात् ॥ ४.२४ ॥
	tad-asaṅkhyeya vāsanābhiḥ citram-api parārtham saṁhatya-kāritvāt
25	विशेषदर्शिन आत्मभावभावनाविनिवृत्तिः ॥ ४.२५ ॥
	viśeṣa-darśinaḥ ātmabhāva-bhāvanā-nivrttiḥ
26	तदा विवेकनिम्नं कैवल्यप्राग्भारं चित्तम् ॥ ४.२६ ॥
	tadā viveka-nimnaṁ kaivalya-prāg-bhāraṁ cittam
27	तच्छिद्रेषु प्रत्ययान्तराणि संस्कारेभ्यः ॥ ४.२७ ॥
	tac-chidreṣu pratyaya-antarāṇi saṁskārebhyaḥ

28	हानमेषां क्लेशवदुक्तम् ॥ ४.२८ ॥
	hānam-eṣāṁ kleśavad-uktam
29	प्रसंख्यानेऽप्यकुसीदस्य सर्वथा विवेकख्यातेर्धर्ममेघः समाधिः ॥ ४.२९ ॥
	prasaṁkhyāne- 'py-akusīdasya sarvathā vivekakhyāteḥ dharma-meghas-samādhiḥ
30	ततः क्लेशकर्मनिवृत्तिः ॥ ४.३० ॥
	tataḥ kleśa-karma-nivrttiḥ
31	तदा सर्वावरणमलापेतस्य ज्ञानस्यानन्त्याज्ज्ञेयमल्पम् ॥ ४.३१ ॥
	tadā sarva-āvaraṇa-malāpetasya jñānasya-ānantyāt jñeyamalpam
32	ततः कृतार्थानां परिणामक्रमसमाप्तिर्गुणानाम् ॥ ४.३२ ॥
	tataḥ krtārthānaṁ pariṇāma-krama-samāptir-guṇānām
33	क्षणप्रतियोगी परिणामापरान्तनिर्ग्राह्यः क्रमः ॥ ४.३३ ॥
	kṣaṇa-pratiyogī pariṇāma-aparānta nirgrāhyaḥ kramaḥ
34	पुरुषार्थशून्यानां गुणानां प्रतिप्रसवः कैवल्यं स्वरूपप्रतिष्ठा वा चितिशक्तिरिति ॥ ४.३४ ॥
	puruṣa-artha-śūnyānāṁ guṇānāṁ-pratiprasavaḥ kaivalyaṁ svarūpa-pratiṣṭhā vā citiśaktiriti

	॥ इति पतञ्जलि-विरचिते योग-सूत्रे चतुर्थः कैवल्य-पादः ॥
	Iti Patanjali-virchite yoga-sutre Chaturtah Kaivalya-padah
	॥ इति श्री पातञ्जल-योग-सूत्राणि ॥
	Iti Shri Patanjala-yoga-sutrani

JAICO PUBLISHING HOUSE

[illegible]

[illegible]

[illegible]

[illegible]